INSTANT DINNERS for BUSY LIFESTYLES

Instant Pot® COOKBOOK

Fast & Easy Recipes that Bring Your Family Back to the Table

BITSY KEOWN

INSTANT POT® COOKBOOK Copyright © 2019 by Bitsy Keown.
All Rights Reserved.

All rights reserved. No part of this book may be reproduced in any form or by any electronic or mechanical means including information storage and retrieval systems, without explicit written permission from the author. The only exception is by a reviewer, who may quote short excerpts in a review of this publication.

Cover and layout designed by: Donna Cunningham; www.beauxarts.design
Editing by: Heather A. O'Connor

Bitsy Keown
Visit my website at www.BitsyKeown.com
and join our community at *Living The Chaos* on Facebook
https://www.facebook.com/livingthechaos

Printed in the United States of America
First Printing: Nov 2019
ISBN: 978-1-70826-165-8

Dedication

*To Momma, for showing me the importance of
dinner together every night.*

Terry, for making me try fried pickles.

*Nicholas & Natalie; may you grow up and enjoy
dinners with your family
as much as I enjoy
spending family dinners with you.*

CONTENTS

INTRODUCTION	9
HOW THE INSTANT POT® JOINED MY FAMILY	11
WATER TEST	13
BEEF RECIPES	15
Beef & Broccoli	17
Beef Fajitas	18
Beef Tips	19
Beef Roast with Potatoes & Carrots	20
Ground Beef Burrito Bowl	21
Korean Beef & Brown Rice	22
Meatloaf & Mashed Potatoes	23
Moo Shu Beef Lettuce Cups	24
Salisbury Steak with Mushroom Gravy	25
Sloppy Joes	27
Stuffed Peppers	28
Swedish Meatballs	29
CHICKEN RECIPES	31
Bourbon Chicken	33
Chicken Cordon Bleu	34
Chicken Enchilada Casserole	35
Chicken Marsala	36
Chicken Teriyaki	37
Chicken Tikka Marsala	38
Creamy Italian Chicken Breast	39
Chicken Breast with Sun-Dried Tomato Cream Sauce	40
Hawaiian BBQ Chicken	41
Honey Balsamic Chicken	42
Thai Lemongrass Chicken	43
Rotisserie Chicken	44
PORK RECIPES	45
Apple Pork Chops	47
Brats & Beer	48
Spiral Honey Ham	49
Honey Mustard Pork Chops	50

BBQ Pulled Pork	51
Pork Adobo	52
Pork BBQ Baby Back Ribs	53
Pork Chile Verde	54
Pork Pot Roast	55
Pork Chops with Creamy Ranch Gravy	56
Sweet Balsamic Pork Loin	57
Thai Moo Wan Sweet Pork	58

SEAFOOD RECIPES   59

Cajun Shrimp & Grits	61
Creamy Herb Parmesan Salmon	62
Drunken Clams	63
Indian Curry Fish	64
Lobster Rolls	65
Low Country Boil	66
Saipan Shrimp	67
Shrimp Fettuccine Alfredo	68
Shrimp Scampi	69
Steamed Alaskan Crab	70
Teriyaki Salmon	71
Tuscan Shrimp	72

BEAN & LEGUME RECIPES   73

Instant Pot Dry Bean Basics	75
Black Beans	77
Cheesy Southwestern Lentils & Brown Rice	78
Chickpea Masala	79
Cowboy Beans	80
Fresh Green Beans & Potatoes	81
Garlic Parmesan Green Beans	82
Green Bean Casserole	83
Buttery Lima Beans with Bacon	84
Refried Beans	85
Red Beans & Rice with Sausage	86
Sugar Snap Peas	87
Tomatillo Poblano White Beans	88

PASTA RECIPES   89

Beef Enchilada Pasta	91
Beef Stroganoff	92
Broccoli & Cheddar Pasta	93
Buffalo Chicken Pasta	94

Butternut Squash Ravioli	95
Cheesy Rosemary Orzo	96
Natalie's Chicken Alfredo Pasta	97
Creamy Chicken Rigatoni	98
Creamy Italian Sausage Tortellini	99
Creamy Ziti	100
Hamburger Mac	101
Chicken Jalapeño Popper Pasta	102
Lemon Parmesan Orzo	103
Macaroni & Cheese	104
Pesto Chicken Pasta	105
Sailor's Garlic Parmesan Pasta	106
Shrimp & Vodka Sauce Pasta	107
Spaghetti & Meat Sauce	108
Spinach & Mushroom Lasagna	109
Taco Pasta	111
Traditional Lasagna	112
Vegetable Lo Mein	114

RICE RECIPES — 115

Basmati & Jasmine White Rice	117
Brown Rice	118
Cajun Rice	119
Cheesy Broccoli & Rice	120
Cilantro Lime Rice	121
Coconut Rice	122
Fried Rice	123
Nick's Garlic Herb Chicken & Rice	124
Quinoa Taco Bowl	125
Perfect Quinoa	126
Rice Pilaf	127
Risotto	128
Turmeric & Garlic Rice	129
Yummy Wild Rice	130
Yellow Rice with Peas & Corn	131

VEGETABLE RECIPES — 133

Bacon Brussel Sprouts	135
Mashed Sweet Potatoes	136
Roasted Butternut Squash	137
Fried Cabbage	138
Coconut Curry Sweet Potatoes	139

Creamy Cheesy Au Gratin Potatoes	140
Delicious Artichokes	141
Easy Golden Beets	142
Eggplant Parmesan	143
Garlic Parmesan Cauliflower	144
Glazed Carrots	145
Lemon Rosemary Asparagus	146
Mashed Cauliflower	147
Mashed Potatoes	148
Parmesan Ranch Corn-on-the-Cob	149
Superfood Kale	150
Perfectly Steamed Broccoli	151
Steamed Spaghetti Squash	152
Spicy Garlic Zucchini	153
Steamed Veggie Mix	154
Twice-Baked Potatoes	155
Zucchini Noodles	156

ELECTRIC PRESSURE COOKER INFORMATION — 157

Liquid Ingredients by Volume	159
Dry Ingredients by Weight	160
Length Comparisons	160
Tips & Information Before Starting	161
What is Pressure Cooking?	161
How to Release Pressure From the Instant Pot	161
Liquid Amounts and Types	161
Warm Up Time	162
Using Other Pans Inside Instant Pot	162
Foods Not to Cook	162
Safety and Cleaning	162
Cleaning Your Instant Pot	163

AUTHOR'S NOTE — 165

Introduction

Hello! I created this cookbook so I could share all my favorite recipes with you. After much coaxing from family and friends, I finally decided to put it all on paper.

Who Am I? Well, I'm just like you, in one area or another. I am a daughter, wife, and mother, who works two jobs from home. Our lives are beyond busy! From work, to after school activities, home management and all the other things we have demanding our attention on a daily basis, who has time to plan the most precious time spent as a family? I know you get it. It gets chaotic at times and the LAST thing we want to do is cook dinner. What's for dinner? When will it be ready? I'm hungry! Stressful daily questions that I would like to make a little easier.

I created this book to get us out of the drive-thru every night and bring our families back to the table. I want to share recipes that have allowed me to do this with my family. Using my Instant Pot has allowed me to cook quality foods in a lot less time and I save money!

I have organized the book with the recipes first, followed by useful tips and information. I set it up in this order because that is my preference. I want to see the recipes without having to read through tons of pages of basic information beforehand; especially, if I already have the basic knowledge of the appliance, utensil or measures. So, The Instant Pot Cookbook; Instant Dinners for Busy Lifestyles is organized a little differently than the classic cookbook. I would like to think that I dare to be different, so there you have it. HA!

I have an Instant Pot <u>Duo Plus 9 in 1, 8- Quart</u> and have tested each of the included recipes. If you are using different sizes and models please, adjustments should be minimal. Also, I use the term pressure cooker, because that's the button on my Instant Pot. Some models read Manual instead, so just be aware that those terms are interchangeable.

Another quick unwritten tip – the Sauté function. My favorite! Sauté seals in the flavor of any meat by slightly searing the outside, while preserving the juicy tenderness of the chosen meat.

A quick note:
The automatic time setting for the Sauté function is 30 minutes, follow the below guideline when using the function:
5 minutes is Low
15 minutes is Medium
30 minutes is High (display will read HOT at full temperature)
PS Don't forget to deglaze! It makes a huge difference in your flavors.

One additional note: Many of the recipes call for chicken or beef broth. If you use vegetarian chicken or beef broth, it would be advised to add a little oil to your water. Otherwise, the lack of any fat in the broth may cause your food to stick to the Instant Pot liner.

All the recipes are 4-6 servings. I wanted to keep that consistent, so it's one less thing to worry about when looking through the recipes.

I have shared just a little about my introduction to pressure-cooking with you and then we'll be on to the BEST part!

How the Instant Pot® Joined My Family

Dinner is better, when we eat together.

When the Instant Pot debuted, I was incredibly intrigued. The latest and greatest. The newest and best! But I had a million questions. Did it really work? Was it hard to use? Would I REALLY use it? I *did* my homework and researched everything I could find about the appliance, the process and results. I was really on the fence about it, but I was so tired of my crockpot. Don't get me wrong, I loved my crockpot, but it always took so LONG to cook anything. If I didn't get something cooking first thing in the morning, I could forget dinner being ready on time.

My biggest struggle was the money. The reviews I found were great, but I am very thrifty and try to be pennywise. Mostly, I was scared of blowing the thing up and wasting my money, making a HUGE mess, or worse an injury. Or, I admit, it becoming a dust collector hidden in the back of my pantry. We have ALL done that, am I right?

My husband saw my angst over the mysterious magical pot and made the decision for me. HAPPY BIRTHDAY to ME! I had my very own Instant Pot. All the recipes I had looked up, bookmarked, mentally prepared, all the meals I was going to create and … it sat in the box for 2 months. Why? I don't know, probably because I was afraid of it.

Fast forward and I am on the way home after picking up my children one afternoon. OHHHHH the moaning and groaning about how starved they are, there is nothing at home, it's the same old thing and nothing would satisfy them but "the drive thru". I was tired after a long chaotic day and relented. We ordered our meals and proceeded to sit in line with at least 10 other cars, while my darling offspring are in the backseat are playing the "he touched me, she looked at me, their breathing too loud" games. Ugh, this is taking forever! FINALLY, food in hand, and as I started to pull off, I realized my order was wrong. Trying really hard to keep my head from spinning around backwards now, I had to get out, go inside and get the order corrected. By the time we headed home, I realized we (I) had endured the torture for OVER 40 minutes!

At that moment, on that drive home, I remembered my Instant Pot. What have I been thinking? I could have prepared AND cooked a complete meal in 10 minutes or less in my Instant Pot. Instead, I wasted time to procure mediocre, processed food, with the end result of each of us splitting off to their own bubble to eat, once home. Let's not forget my stress level was off the charts. Had I not been so afraid to try the mysterious appliance, I would, in that very moment, be sitting at the table with my family.

The very next day, I got over myself, and pulled my Instant Pot out of the box. I performed the water test, then made the best Chicken and Rice Recipe! In 6 minutes, I had dinner on the table, and my dining room was filled with excitement. We talked about our days, we laughed, we told jokes and we ATE TOGETHER. It was surreal for me. This time together was what I was missing and had not taken the time to even notice. I had been so caught up in life's hectic schedule, that I forgotten how much I enjoyed the quality time with the ones I love.

Since then, I have cooked hundreds of meals, and it always makes me smile. I reflect on how dinner was such a pain for me, and how my Instant Pot turned it all around. We are now creating memories. That is exactly what I hope to share with you. I want you to be able to be able to sit down for dinner with your family and just have fun together.

Water Test

It's really not that scary.

"What would life be if we had no courage to attempt anything?"
–Vincent van Gogh

As I shared my fears about even using the Instant Pot, I am so embarrassed to even tell this story. We are friends now, so I will share. I really am not this goofy, or weirdo, well.... maybe I am! I mentioned before that using my Instant Pot scared the *bazinga* out of me and it was my fear alone that was holding me back. After the "drive thru" revelation, I was determined to brave the Instant Pot. I could do it! My family deserved it. So here we go, determined to master the mystery of pressure cooking and visualizing my family sitting at the same table; at the same time sharing the same meal. I read the instruction manual cover to cover and discovered the Water Test.

Purpose of the Water Test

1. To test the Instant Pot is working correctly.
2. To create comfort in using the pot.

Water Test Instructions

1. Pour 3 cups of water into the inner pot of your instant pot.
2. Put the lid on and turn your valve to seal.
3. Set to high pressure for 3 minutes. You do this by hitting the pressure cook button and then plus or minus until the screens reads "3."
4. Once pressure is reached, the instant pot will begin to count down from 3 minutes to 0.
5. Once the time is done, the Instant Pot will beep and will turn to the "keep warm" function.
6. To turn your instant pot off, hit the off button and your pot will read "off."
7. Let pressure release and then remove lid and dump out water.

I put on my big girl pants and began the water test process. Images of exploding water, in geyser fashion, dance in my head. I keep thinking I am going to be scalded with boiling hot water, because I have that kind of luck. How will I protect myself from this process? I've got it! An umbrella! Yeah.. here comes the embarrassing part...

Visualize with me, I have an open, U-Shape kitchen and the Instant Pot is sitting on the bar by the sink. I press the pressure cook button, set the 3 minutes, and run to the opposite side of the kitchen as if a bomb was about to go off. I bravely opened the umbrella, and placed it in front of me, facing the direction of the Instant Pot. I swear I looked like Captain America with his shield ready for battle. I gripped the handle of the umbrella so tightly, that the design of the handle imprinted on my hand. One minute passes, no explosion, and I got bored. (You know, watched pot never boils) I was starting to feel more relaxed, so to pass the time, I decided to "Sing in the Rain" ... and dance around the kitchen with my umbrella. When the Instant Pot beeped at 3 minutes, it startled out of my musical interpretation and I whipped around with my umbrella as my shield and nearly knocking the pot off the counter!!

Carefully, I approached the Instant Pot, looked at the display and the water test was complete... DONE... no explosion, no catastrophic, shooting of boiling water, NOTHING. Simply a beep. I am mentally kicking myself now. Why was I so afraid? It had worked perfectly! Yet, there I was in the kitchen with an umbrella as my shield like an idiot. I began laughing until I needed a tissue. So began a new era in my kitchen.

Now let's get to the good stuff! The recipes! The chapters are organized by different food types, so if you want chicken, then you go straight to the chicken chapter. Look for the labels at the bottom of the page; they will help you know which chapter you are in should you happen to be just flipping through the pages.

My family and friends have tried each recipe. Sometimes I told them I was testing Instant Pot recipes; sometimes I did not, to get true results of the recipes. The recipes are easy, quick, and delicious. I hope you and your family enjoy them, personalize them for your taste, and have your own *"Sing in the Rain"* party.

Beef Recipes

Cooking is like painting or writing a song. Just as there are only so many notes or colors, there are only so many flavors - it's how you combine them that sets you apart.

-Wolfgang Puck

Beef & Broccoli

This is my go-to recipe when I want Chinese food without having to order take-out.

PREP 3 MIN | COOK 10 MIN | NATURAL RELEASE

INGREDIENTS

3 Tablespoons olive oil

1.5 Pounds thinly sliced steak

1 small onion

3 cloves garlic

1 medium broccoli crown

3/4 Cup beef broth

1/3 Cup soy sauce

1/3 Cup brown sugar

Optional

1 Tablespoon cornstarch

2 Tablespoons water

INSTRUCTIONS

1. Press Sauté button and add olive oil. Once pot is hot, add sliced steak and brown about 2 minutes.

2. Add in onions and garlic, continue to sauté until onions are tender.

3. Add broccoli, beef broth, soy sauce and brown sugar and stir until sugar is dissolved.

4. Put on lid, select pressure cook, add 10 minutes at high pressure. Once completed, Natural Release and once button drops, remove lid.

5. Optional: If sauce isn't thick enough, return pot to sauté mode and mix 2 tablespoons water with 1 tablespoon cornstarch and add to sauce. Let boil 1-2 minutes.

6. Note: If you would like firmer broccoli, steam in pot first, and add to sauce after pressure cooking steak & sauce.

Beef Fajitas

Classic fajitas recipe, made with strips of skirt steak, onions and bell peppers, and serve with fresh tortillas, guacamole, sour cream, and salsa.

PREP 10 MIN | COOK 15 MIN | QUICK RELEASE

INGREDIENTS

2 Tablespoons canola oil

2 bell peppers, sliced

1 onion, sliced

2 Tablespoons garlic, minced

1 Pound beef skirt steak, sliced

1 jalapeño minced

1 Teaspoon cumin

1 Teaspoons chili powder

1/2 Teaspoons smoked paprika

¼ Cup beef broth

INSTRUCTIONS

1. Add canola oil into your pot, then add garlic, onion and peppers.

2. Press Sauté button and cook for 2 minutes, until onion are golden.

3. Add steak, jalapeño, cumin, chili powder, and smoked paprika, stir well to let the flavors combine. Stir for another minute.

4. Pour in beef broth, then put on lid and seal.

5. Press Pressure Cook button, add 8 minutes at high pressure.

6. When complete, Quick Release the steam carefully.

7. Pair mixture in flour tortillas and top with salsa, cheese, sour cream, or your favorite toppings.

Beef Tips

Tender beef cooked in a delicious gravy, can be served over rice, mashed potatoes or egg noodles. Simple to make comfort food that the whole family will love.

PREP 5 MIN | COOK 30 MIN | NATURAL RELEASE

INGREDIENTS

2 Pounds sirloin beef tips

3 Tablespoons flour

1/2 Tablespoon garlic salt

1/2 Teaspoons black pepper

2 to 4 Tablespoons olive oil

1/4 Cup onions, diced

1 Cup beef broth

1/2 Cup red wine

10.5oz can cream of mushroom soup

Optional

1/4 Cup water

2 Tablespoons cornstarch

INSTRUCTIONS

1. Season sirloin beef tips with garlic salt, pepper and dust with flour.

2. Set the pot to sauté and let it get hot. Add oil. Place in the sirloin beef tips and sauté until browned. Remove beef tips.

3. Add in the onion and sauté about 1 minute.

4. Pour in red wine and beef broth. Deglaze the pan and get the bits off the bottom of pan. Return Beef Tips and juices back into pot. Stir and add cream of mushroom on top.

5. Close the lid and make sure the pressure valve is closed. (I forget this ALL the time!) Use the Pressure Cook button on High Pressure for 25 minutes. Once done let it release naturally.

6. If gravy is not as thick as you desire take 1/4 cup water with 2 tablespoons of cornstarch until well mixed. Pour into pot and stir. Set sauté and let bubble a few minutes until thickened.

Beef Roast with Potatoes & Carrots

Tender, juicy, and packed with flavor.
The perfect Sunday dinner to bring the family together!

PREP 15 MIN | COOK 50 MIN | NATURAL RELEASE

INGREDIENTS

2 to 3 Pound roast

1 Teaspoon minced Garlic

1/2 Teaspoon Italian Seasoning

1/2 Teaspoon salt

1/2 Teaspoon pepper

4 Cups beef broth

1.5 Pounds any potatoes of your choice

4 carrots peeled

½ medium onion

Gravy

1/4 Cup water for the gravy

2 Tablespoons cornstarch

INSTRUCTIONS

1. Add roast to the pot first; add all the seasonings, then the beef broth.

2. Put the lid on and set it to sealing. Use the Pressure Cook button at high pressure setting for 50 minutes and when complete, allow to natural release.

3. While the roast is cooking, cut all your vegetables into large chunks. You want them to be bigger so they will not turn into mush.

4. After this cooking time, remove the beef.

5. Next add your vegetables to the pot (with the beef juices) and cook on high pressure for 10 minutes with a quick release. Remove the vegetables from the pot after this cooking time.

6. Now, to make the gravy. Change the instant pot setting to the sauté feature.

7. In a small bowl whisk together the 1/4 cup of water and the cornstarch.

8. Whisk in the water and cornstarch mixture in with the beef juice in the instant pot.

9. Bring to a boil, stirring frequently for 3-5 minutes until it begins to thicken. Drizzle the gravy over the roast, potatoes, and carrots.

Ground Beef Burrito Bowl

This easy beef burrito bowl is one of my favorites and it comes together quickly. It is loaded with southwest flavor, and keeps me full for hours. It will become a regular in your meal rotation.

PREP 5 MIN | COOK 10 MIN | QUICK RELEASE

INGREDIENTS

1 Pound ground beef
3 Tablespoons olive oil
1/2 yellow onion minced
1 Teaspoon garlic powder
1 Teaspoon onion powder
1/2 Teaspoon smoked paprika
2 Teaspoons chili powder
1 1/2 Teaspoons cumin
1/4 Teaspoon ground coriander
1/4 Teaspoon oregano
1 Cup uncooked extra-long grain rice
14.5oz can fire roasted diced tomatoes with diced green chilies drained
15oz can black beans drained and rinsed
1 Cup frozen corn
2 1/4 Cups Beef Broth
1 Cup of shredded jack cheese

Toppings:
Cheese
Tomatoes, chopped
Avocado, chopped
Sour cream
Jalapeño, sliced

INSTRUCTIONS

1. Press the Sauté button. Once hot, add ground beef to the pot, using a wooden spoon to break up the meat.

2. Add 2 tablespoons of olive oil and the onions and seasonings and cook until onions start to soften.

3. Add an additional tablespoon of olive oil and uncooked rice and toast rice for a minute.

4. Stir in black beans, canned tomatoes, corn, and broth.

5. Lock pot lid in place, select Pressure Cook at High Pressure for 7 minutes.

6. Use Quick Release, and once pressure button drops, open pot and fluff the rice.

7. Sprinkle with the cheese, recover for 1-2 minutes to melt cheese.

8. Garnish with toppings.

Korean Beef & Brown Rice

A delicious, quick, easy, and budget-friendly dinner.

PREP 10 MIN | COOK 22 MIN | QUICK RELEASE

INGREDIENTS

4 cloves garlic, chopped

1/2 Cup beef broth

1/2 Cup soy sauce

3 1/2 Tablespoon light brown sugar

1 Tablespoon rice vinegar

1 Tablespoon Gochujang, plus more for serving (Korean Chili Paste)

1 Teaspoons toasted sesame oil

1 Pound beef stew meat

2 Cups long grain brown rice

2 1/2 Cups + 2 Tablespoons water

1 Tablespoon cornstarch

2 Teaspoons white sesame seeds

Chopped Green Onions, for serving

INSTRUCTIONS

1. To make sauce, stir together garlic, beef broth, soy sauce, light brown sugar, rice vinegar, Gochujang, and toasted sesame oil.
2. Combine sauce and beef in the base of the Instant Pot.
3. Place a metal rack on top of the beef.
4. Combine rice and 2 ½ cups water in a bowl that is approved for use in the Instant Pot. Place the bowl on top of the rack.
5. Close and lock the lid.
6. Set the Pressure Cook button on high for 22 minutes.
7. Allow the pressure to release naturally for 10 minutes.
8. Carefully remove the rack and bowl of rice and set them aside.
9. Change the pot setting to Sauté
10. Whisk together cornstarch and 2 Tablespoon of water. Slowly pour cornstarch / water mixture over beef. Stir constantly, until sauce thickens about 2 minutes.
11. Serve the beef and sauce over rice with sesame seeds and green onions on top. Serve extra gochujang on the side if desired.

MEATLOAF & MASHED POTATOES

A meat-and-potato lover's delight. It's a quick hearty meal and great to take for a potluck dinner.

PREP 20 MIN | COOK 15 MIN | NATURAL RELEASE

INGREDIENTS

2 pounds lean ground beef

1/2 Cups panko breadcrumbs

1/3 Cup whole milk

1 small yellow onion, diced very small

1 large egg, lightly beaten

1 Teaspoon kosher salt

2 Tablespoons Dijon mustard

2 pounds large Yukon gold potatoes, peeled and quartered

2 Cups water

1/2 Teaspoon kosher salt

1/4 Cup ketchup

2 Tablespoons packed light brown sugar

1 Cup half-and-half

4 Tablespoons unsalted butter

INSTRUCTIONS

1. Place the ground beef, breadcrumbs, milk, onion, egg, and salt in a large bowl. Use your hands to gently combine until mixed thoroughly. Shape the meat mixture into a loaf, about 6 inches long and 4 inches wide, and set inside a 6-inch round cake pan; set aside.

2. Combine the potatoes, water, and salt in the Instant Pot insert and stir to combine. Place a trivet over the potatoes.

3. Create a sling for the meatloaf pan by folding a 12-inch long piece of aluminum foil lengthwise into a 3-inch wide strip. Place the meatloaf pan in the center of the strip and then fold up the sides — you should have 3 to 4 inches of overhang (handles) on either side.

4. Lower the meatloaf pan into the Instant Pot and place on top of the trivet. Seal the Instant Pot and set to Pressure Cook on High Pressure for 35 minutes. While the meatloaf cooks, arrange a rack in the middle of the oven and heat to 400°F. Stir the ketchup, brown sugar, and mustard together in a small bowl to make the glaze.

5. When the cook time is over, let the Instant Pot naturally release pressure for 10 minutes. Manually release any remaining pressure. Open the Instant Pot and use the foil sling to carefully remove the meatloaf. Carefully drain off the fat and juices around the meatloaf. Brush the meatloaf with the glaze and bake until it is glossy and caramelized, 8 to 10 minutes.

6. While the meatloaf bakes, add the half-and-half and butter to the potatoes and mash to desired consistency. Slice the meatloaf and serve with the mashed potatoes.

Moo Shu Beef Lettuce Cups

I love how flavorful this recipe turns out, and wrapping it up in lettuce keeps it low-carb. It's great for portion control too, because you can only fit so much meat into one lettuce leaf.

PREP 5 MIN | COOK 35 MIN | NATURAL RELEASE

INGREDIENTS

1 Tablespoon butter

2 eggs slightly beaten

3 Tablespoons olive oil

2 Tablespoons garlic minced

2 Pound chuck roast

1/4 Cup rice wine vinegar

1/2 Cup hoisin sauce

1/2 Cup soy sauce

1 Tablespoon sesame oil

1 Teaspoon ground ginger

1 Tablespoon brown sugar

1 pint of sliced mushrooms

2 1/2 Cups coleslaw mix

One head of lettuce

Salt and pepper to taste

INSTRUCTIONS

1. Set Instant Pot to sauté. When hot, add butter and allow to sizzle. Add eggs and cook for 1-2 minutes until eggs begin to firm. Flip eggs and cook an additional 30 seconds. Remove, cut into thin strips and set aside. Cancel sauté, remove inner liner, wipe it clean, and then return it to the Instant Pot.

2. Set Instant Pot to sauté. When hot, add olive oil and garlic. Cook 1-2 minutes. Add beef and brown on each side.

3. In a small bowl, add vinegar, hoisin and soy sauces, sesame oil, ginger, and brown sugar. Whisk together and reserve 1/4 cup. Pour remainder of sauce into Instant Pot, covering the beef.

4. Set Instant Pot on Pressure Cook at High Pressure for 35 minutes. When the cook time ends, let the pressure release naturally for 15 minutes.

5. After 15 minutes, turn valve to venting to release remaining pressure. When pressure is fully released, remove the lid. Using two forks, shred beef.

6. Add mushrooms and 2 cups of the coleslaw mix to the beef in the Instant Pot. Secure lid, turn valve to sealing, press Manual and set Instant Pot to high pressure for 3 minutes. Allow to release pressure naturally for 5 minutes, then quick release remaining pressure. Turn off Instant Pot.

7. Serve over rice or add 2 tablespoons of Moo Shu Beef to individual lettuce cups. Top Moo Shu Beef with a few slices of egg and coleslaw mix. Drizzle sauce.

Salisbury Steak with Mushroom Gravy

One of those comfort food favorites that never goes out of style. It's quick to make, inexpensive, and is popular with kids and adults. This homemade version is WAY better than the kind you'll typically find in the grocery freezer section.

PREP 15 MIN | COOK 5 MIN | NATURAL RELEASE

INGREDIENTS

2 Tablespoon olive oil

2 large onions, finely chopped

SALISBURY STEAK PATTIES

1.5 Pounds ground beef

1 egg, beaten

2 Teaspoons garlic, crushed

1 Tablespoon tomato paste

1 Teaspoons Worcestershire sauce

1 Tablespoon beef broth concentrate

2 Teaspoons mustard powder

1/2 Teaspoon salt

1/2 Teaspoon pepper

1 Tablespoon dried minced onions

1/2 Cup cooked onion, taken from 2 onions listed above

INSTRUCTIONS

1. Turn on the sauté function in your Instant pot and add olive oil and the finely chopped onions. Cook until soft and a little golden in color, about 5 minutes then remove from the pot and measure out 1/2 cup to add to the Salisbury steak patties.

2. In a large bowl add ground beef, beaten egg, garlic, tomato paste, Worcestershire sauce, beef broth concentrate, tomato paste, mustard powder, salt, pepper, dried minced onions, 1/2 cup of the cooked onions, Panko breadcrumbs, and mix well.

3. Form into 8 patties and then turn on the sauté function button, add a little olive oil and brown the patties on both sides. Remove the patties and set aside.

4. Add the beef broth to the Instant pot and deglaze the bottom of the pan well so that nothing is left sticking to the base.

5. Add the gravy ingredients to the pot including all the remaining cooked onion, Worcestershire sauce, tomato paste, dried minced onion, and stir well to combine.

6. Add the Salisbury steak patties into the gravy then add the lid and lock. Turn the steam release vent to seal and use the Pressure Cook setting, adjust it to cook for 6 minutes at High Pressure.

7. When complete, release steam naturally which will take about 12-15 minutes or until the pin drops, then remove

1/2 Cup panko breadcrumbs

INSTANT POT SALISBURY STEAK GRAVY

2 Cups beef broth

add remaining cooked onion

1 Teaspoons Worcestershire sauce

1 Tablespoon. tomato paste

2 Tablespoons dried minced onion

2 Teaspoons cornstarch

1 Tablespoon cold water

1/2 Pound mushrooms, sliced

the lid. Carefully remove the Salisbury Steak Patties and set aside and cover with foil.

8. Mix the cornstarch with 1tbsp cold water and add to the gravy and stir thoroughly.

9. Add the sliced mushrooms to the gravy and continue to stir. Let simmer for a few minutes until the gravy has thickened and the mushrooms are cooked. Add back the patties to the gravy, serve hot with mashed potatoes, rice or pasta.

SLOPPY JOES

This recipe is super-versatile. You can use carrots and celery instead of a bell pepper, sweeten the Joes with brown sugar for more sweetness, or add chili powder and red pepper if you like a spicier filling.

PREP 15 MIN | COOK 15 MIN | NATURAL RELEASE

INGREDIENTS

1 Tablespoons olive oil

2 Pounds ground beef

Salt and pepper

1 yellow onion diced small

1 red bell pepper diced small

Sauce

8oz tomato sauce

2 Tablespoons tomato paste

1/2 Cup ketchup

1/2 Cup BBQ sauce

1 1/2 Tablespoons Worcestershire Sauce

1 Tablespoons yellow mustard

1 Teaspoons garlic powder

1 Cup beef broth

INSTRUCTIONS

1. Turn instant pot on to sauté function and add olive oil to the bottom of the pan
2. Add ground beef, onions, and red pepper, and sauté and brown the ground beef. This should take 5-7 minutes.
3. Once browned, add all sauce ingredients. Stir well.
4. Put lid on, and lock into place.
5. Set valve to sealing.
6. Set pressure to Pressure Cook at High Pressure for 5 minutes.
7. After the 5 minutes, let pressure naturally release for 10 minutes. Then quick release any remaining pressure.
8. Stir pot, and if sauce needs to reduce, turn on to sauté, and cook until desired thickness is reached.

Stuffed Peppers

My friends often ask me how to make stuffed bell peppers and my response is always the same – it's so easy! While these may look difficult, if you follow these easy steps, you will have perfect stuffed peppers every time.

PREP 15 MIN | COOK 9 MIN | NATURAL RELEASE

INGREDIENTS

4 Medium bell peppers

1 Small onion

½ Pound ground beef

2 Cups rice, cooked, packed

1½ Tablespoon marjoram

1 Teaspoon salt

¼ Teaspoon black pepper

2 Cloves garlic

3 Tablespoon breadcrumbs

14 oz Can tomatoes

½ Cup water

INSTRUCTIONS

1. Rinse the peppers. Cut off the top parts and remove all the membranes and seeds.

2. In a bowl, combine together finely chopped onion, ground beef, cooked rice, marjoram, salt, pepper, minced garlic, breadcrumbs and ½ can of tomatoes (without their juice). Mix well using your hand or spoon.

3. Fill each pepper with the mixture.

4. Add water and the remaining tomatoes (with juices) to the inner pot of the Instant pot. Insert the steam rack and place the stuffed peppers onto it.

5. Lock the lid. Turn the steam release to seal and Select Pressure Cook. Adjust the time to 8 minutes on High Pressure. Let the pressure release before opening the lid.

6. To avoid peppers falling apart, let them cool slightly before serving.

Swedish Meatballs

Nothing beats homemade meatballs smothered in a creamy gravy.

PREP 10 MIN | COOK 8 MIN | QUICK RELEASE

INGREDIENTS

10.75oz Can cream of mushroom soup

10.75oz Can golden mushroom soup

14oz Can beef broth

1 envelope brown gravy mix

2 Cups water

3 Cups egg noodles dry

24oz Frozen Meatballs

1 Cups sour cream

INSTRUCTIONS

1. In the pressure cooker combine the soups, broth, gravy mix and water. Whisk together until combined. Stir in egg noodles and meatballs.

2. Place lid on Instant Pot and make sure vent is sealed.

3. Select Pressure Cook at High pressure for 8 minutes. Quick release pressure.

4. Stir in sour cream until combined.

Chicken Recipes

The most indispensable ingredient of all good home cooking,
is love for those you are cooking for.

-Sophia Loren

Bourbon Chicken

Bourbon chicken is a dish named after Bourbon Street in New Orleans, Louisiana and for the bourbon whiskey ingredient. The dish is commonly found at Cajun-themed establishments.

PREP 5 MIN | COOK 20 MIN | QUICK RELEASE

INGREDIENTS

- **1/2 Cup apple juice**
- **1/2 Cup Bourbon**
- **1/4 Cup soy sauce**
- **1/2 Cup light brown sugar**
- **1/4 Cup ketchup**
- **2 Tablespoon honey**
- **1/2 Teaspoon crushed red pepper flakes**
- **4 Cloves garlic, pressed**
- **1/2 Teaspoon ginger**
- **2 Pounds boneless, skinless chicken thighs (or breasts)**
- **3 Tablespoon cornstarch**
- **3 Tablespoon water**
- **3 green onions, sliced**

INSTRUCTIONS

1. In the bottom of your instant pot, start adding your ingredients. Apple juice, Bourbon, soy sauce, brown sugar, ketchup, honey, crushed red pepper flakes, fresh garlic, and ginger. Use a whisk and mix it really good. Place your chicken into the instant pot, making sure it's coated in the bourbon mixture.

2. Secure the lid to your pressure cooker, and turn the release valve to seal. Turn on the Instant Pot and press Pressure Cook on High Pressure. Set the timer for 12 minutes (or 18 minutes if using frozen chicken).

3. While it's cooking, mix your cornstarch and cold water in a small bowl until combined.

4. Once the chicken is done cooking, allow it to naturally release for 5 minutes. Then do a quick release.

5. Remove your chicken from the instant pot and place it on a cutting board. Dice into bite sized pieces.

6. Turn your pressure cooker to sauté and slowly add in the cornstarch mixture. Using your whisk, mix continuously until thickened. This takes about two minutes. Turn pressure cooker off and return chicken to the sauce. Top with green onions.

Chicken Cordon Bleu

This classic French dish, more than lives up to its name, which means blue ribbon. It's also far easier to make than you may think. Great option for kids; mine love it.

PREP 12 MIN | COOK 15 MIN | QUICK RELEASE

INGREDIENTS

2 Cups panko breadcrumbs

1 Teaspoon salt

1/2 Teaspoon pepper

3-4 chicken breast halves boneless, skinless

8 slices deli ham thinly sliced

4 slices Swiss cheese

1/2 Cup butter melted

1 Cup chicken broth

INSTRUCTIONS

1. In a shallow dish, combine Panko, salt, and pepper. Set aside.

2. Pound chicken breast to 1/2" thickness Place 2 slices of ham over each chicken breast. (Awesome stress reliever HA!)

3. Place slice of Swiss cheese over the ham and roll chicken up tightly.

4. Dip each chicken roll in butter, then roll in breadcrumbs. Place in Instant Pot, seam side down (the more snug the better).

5. If you don't want your chicken sitting in broth, you may want to use the included steamer rack so the chicken isn't sitting on the bottom of the pot.

6. Pour remaining butter over the chicken and add chicken broth in the cracks between the chicken breasts.

7. Place lid on Instant Pot and turn value to sealing. Select Pressure cook button and set time to 8 minutes, on high pressure. Allow to naturally release for 5 minutes then Quick Release the remaining pressure.

8. Carefully remove chicken from Instant Pot and serve.

Chicken Enchilada Casserole

We could eat Mexican dishes every night of the week. This is an easy recipe for the Mexican food lover in your home.

PREP 20 MIN | COOK 20 MIN | NATURAL RELEASE

INGREDIENTS

1 Tablespoon of vegetable oil plus additional for toasting tortillas

1 cup of finely diced onion

4 cloves of garlic minced

1 jalapeño seeds removed, minced

1 cup chicken broth

2 (8 oz.) cans of tomato sauce

2 tablespoons of chili powder

1 tablespoon of sugar

1 teaspoon of cumin

1 teaspoon of kosher salt and several turns of freshly ground pepper

1 1/2 pounds of boneless skinless chicken breasts

2 tablespoons of chopped fresh cilantro plus more for garnish

12 corn tortillas

8 oz. of sharp cheddar cheese shredded

8 oz. of Monterey jack cheese shredded

Sour cream for serving

INSTRUCTIONS

1. Set Instant Pot to Sauté and add 1 tablespoon of oil.

2. Sauté onions, garlic and jalapeño until onions start to soften and turn translucent, 2-3 minutes.

3. Add chicken broth, tomato sauce, chili powder, sugar, cumin, salt and pepper to Instant Pot and stir to combine.

4. Add chicken breasts to Instant Pot, close lid and set pressure release valve to Sealing.

5. Set Instant Pot to High Pressure from Pressure Cook Button for 10 minutes.

6. While chicken breasts and sauce are cooking, shred cheese and prepare tortillas.

7. To prepare tortillas, preheat oven to 400 degrees.

8. Brush tortillas lightly with vegetable oil, spread on a baking sheet and heat in oven for about 5 minutes, just until soft and pliable.

9. Once chicken is completed, let steam release naturally. Open lid carefully and add chicken and toppings.

Chicken Marsala

Surprisingly, I discovered that my kids like mushrooms and starting looking for ideas to use them. Anytime they "like" something I try to incorporate it wherever I can. This is one of the meals that made them run to the table!

PREP 15 MIN | COOK 10 MIN | NATURAL RELEASE

INGREDIENTS

2 boneless skinless chicken breasts

Salt & Pepper

1 Tablespoon olive oil

10oz fresh mushrooms sliced

3 Cloves garlic minced

1/2 Cup dry marsala wine (or cooking marsala)

1/2 Cup heavy whipping cream

1 Tablespoon fresh lemon juice

1 Tablespoon corn starch

1/2 Teaspoon dried oregano

Chopped fresh parsley

INSTRUCTIONS

1. Butterfly each chicken breast to make it thinner. Sprinkle all over with salt and pepper.

2. Select the sauté mode on the pressure cooker. Add olive oil to coat the bottom of the pot. When the display reads HOT, add garlic and mushrooms, cooking for a few minutes until they start to release their juices, stirring frequently. Turn off the sauté mode.

3. Add Marsala wine and briefly scrape up any brown bits stuck to the bottom of the pot.

4. Add heavy cream, lemon juice, and oregano, and stir everything together. Add chicken on top of the mushrooms, arranging the chicken in a single layer if possible. Press down on the chicken pieces so they're barely submerged in the wine sauce.

5. Secure the lid and seal the vent. Select the Pressure Cook button and cook for 4 minutes at high pressure. As soon as it's done, naturally release the pressure.

6. Uncover and transfer only the chicken to a plate.

7. Turn on the sauté mode. In a small bowl, combine corn starch with 2 tablespoons of cold water and stir until dissolved. Add to the pot and simmer for a few minutes to thicken the sauce a bit, stirring frequently. Turn off the sauté mode.

8. Add the chicken back to the pot to let it briefly soak up the sauce. Serve while hot and garnish with chopped fresh parsley.

Chicken Teriyaki

If you're not in the mood to head to the mall, but you're craving that plate of "mall food court" Chicken Teriyaki, then you're going to love this recipe.

PREP 10 MIN | COOK 15 MIN | NATURAL RELEASE

INGREDIENTS

Teriyaki Sauce:

½ **Cup low sodium soy sauce**

¼ **Cup rice vinegar**

2 Cloves garlic, minced

2 Teaspoons fresh grated ginger

2 Tablespoons canola oil

2 Tablespoons honey

¼ **Teaspoon black pepper**

1 Tablespoon corn starch

2 Tablespoons canola oil

6-8 boneless, skinless chicken thighs

1 green onion, sliced

Sesame seeds, for garnish (optional)

INSTRUCTIONS

1. Combine teriyaki sauce ingredients in a mixing bowl. Set aside.

2. Heat the Instant Pot in Sauté mode. Add oil and brown the chicken, about 2-3 minutes per side. When the chicken is browned press Cancel.

3. Add the teriyaki sauce to the pot; mix to combine.

4. Cover and lock the lid. Select Pressure Cook and adjust the time to 10 minutes. When the time is over, let the pressure release on its own for 5 minutes. Then, carefully turn the valve to Venting, to release any extra pressure that might still be in there.

5. Sprinkle with sliced green onions and sesame seeds, if desired. Serve with rice or quinoa.

Chicken Tikka Marsala

If there's one dish guaranteed to be on every Indian restaurant menu, it is chicken tikka masala, which is composed of chunks of chicken enveloped in a creamy spiced tomato sauce.

PREP 15 MIN | COOK 10 MIN | QUICK RELEASE

INGREDIENTS

CHICKEN MARINADE
1 ½ Pounds boneless skinless chicken breasts (or thighs), cut into 1 inch cubes
½ Cup plain yogurt
1 Tablespoon lemon juice
3 Cloves garlic, grated or minced
1 Teaspoon EACH:
Grated ginger
Garam masala
¼ Teaspoon ground white pepper

TIKKA MASALA
1 Tablespoon olive oil
1 (15-ounce) can tomato
1 ½ Teaspoon grated ginger
8 Cloves garlic, grated or minced
2 Teaspoons dried fenugreek leaves
1 Teaspoon EACH:
ground cumin, ground coriander, smoked paprika, garam masala
½ Teaspoon ground turmeric
¼ – ½ Teaspoon cayenne pepper
½ Cup heavy cream
Cooked basmati rice
Chopped cilantro, for serving

INSTRUCTIONS

1. MARINATE THE CHICKEN: In a medium bowl, whisk together the yogurt, lemon juice, ginger paste, garlic paste, ground white pepper, 1 teaspoon salt, and garam masala. Add the diced chicken and mix; set aside for at least 20 minutes. If you've got time, I put in a Ziploc bag and letting it hang out in the refrigerator for 1-10 hours.

2. SAUTÉ: Select the sauté mode on your instant pot when it's hot, add the oil followed by the marinated chicken (along with the marinade) and let sauté for 2-3 minutes, stirring so nothing sticks to the bottom.

3. PRESSURE COOK: Add all of the remaining ingredients for the sauce (except the cream) along with ½ teaspoon salt and stir everything well. Cover with the lid, make sure valve is on sealing and Pressure Cook on high pressure for 9 minutes. Use the quick release to release the steam as soon as the timer goes off.

4. FINISH: Hit the sauté button and drizzle in the cream; stir to combine. When the tikka masala reaches a gentle simmer. Turn off and serve warm with cooked rice topped with chopped cilantro.

Creamy Italian Chicken Breast

These Creamy Italian Instant Pot Chicken Breasts are wonderful! They cook in just minutes and are coated in a creamy sauce of Italian herbs and roasted red peppers.

PREP 10 MIN | COOK 8 MIN | NATURAL RELEASE

INGREDIENTS

4 boneless skinless chicken breasts

1 Cup low sodium chicken broth

1 Teaspoon minced garlic

1 Teaspoon Italian seasoning

1/4 Teaspoon salt

1/4 Teaspoon black pepper

1/3 Cup heavy cream

1/3 Cup chopped roasted red peppers

1 1/2 Tablespoons corn starch

1 Tablespoon basil pesto

INSTRUCTIONS

1. Place chicken breasts in the bottom of the Instant Pot. Add broth and sprinkle with garlic, Italian seasoning, salt and pepper.

2. Place lid on the Instant Pot and turn valve to sealing. Select Pressure Cook at High Pressure, and set the timer to 8 minutes.

3. Once the cook time is over, turn the Instant Pot off and let pressure release naturally for 5 minutes, then do a quick release and open the lid.

4. Remove the chicken breasts and place on a cutting board or serving platter. Turn the Instant Pot to sauté. (OPTIONAL: strain the broth if there is fat or unappetizing chunks left over)

5. Stir together cream, red peppers, corn starch and pesto and add to the pot. Whisk and cook for 3-4 minutes, until thickened. Add chicken back to the sauce or serve with the sauce over top if desired.

Chicken Breast with Sun-Dried Tomato Cream Sauce

Cooking is one of my favorite hobbies. My husband and I like to create new recipes and pair our creations with a nice wine. Sometimes we have to readjust our recipes, but this one comes out amazing every time.

PREP 10 MIN | COOK 20 MIN | QUICK RELEASE

INGREDIENTS

1 Pound boneless skinless chicken breasts

1 Cup chicken broth

1/3 Cup sun dried tomatoes,

drained, chopped finely

1/2 Teaspoon dried basil

1/2 Teaspoon dried oregano

1/4 Teaspoon red pepper flakes optional; adds a bit of spice

2 Cloves garlic minced

After reducing the sauce

1/2 Cup parmesan cheese grated

3/4 Cup heavy cream

INSTRUCTIONS

1. In the Instant Pot, combine the chicken stock, sun dried tomatoes, basil, oregano, red pepper flakes, garlic and chicken breasts.

2. Cook on high pressure for 8 minutes, using the Pressure Cook Button.

3. When cooking is complete, Quick Release the pressure and carefully transfer the chicken breasts to a cutting board to rest.

4. Select the Sauté function, and allow cooking liquids to simmer for 7 or so minutes, until reduced to about 1/3 of a cup and you can see the bottom of the pot as you stir.

5. Stir in the parmesan cheese and heavy cream until completely combined and heated throughout (do not boil).

6. Slice the chicken and add back to the pot, or simply spoon the sauce over the chicken breast.

Hawaiian BBQ Chicken

Just getting home after a long day at work and running taxi service all over with the kids? Hawaiian BBQ Chicken will give your family a nice dinner, with little effort. Especially on nights you just don't feel like cooking. It is excellent left over the next day for lunch in a wrap or topping a salad.

PREP 5 MIN | COOK 12 MIN | QUICK RELEASE

INGREDIENTS

2 boneless skinless chicken breasts

1 cup pineapple chunks

1/2 cup pineapple juice

1.5 cups BBQ sauce

INSTRUCTIONS

1. Place chicken breasts on the bottom of the instant pot. Add pineapple juice and stir. Arrange pineapple chunks over chicken and alongside, make sure no chunks are under the chicken.

2. Pour BBQ sauce over chicken. DO NOT STIR.

3. Place lid on your Instant Pot, switch the valve to sealing position. Press Pressure Cook button and adjust timer to 12 minutes at High Pressure.

4. When the timer is done, carefully, switch the valve to vent to Quick Release pressure.

5. Remove chicken breast onto a cutting board and shred with two forks.

6. Return chicken to IP and stir with the sauce.

7. If the sauce is too runny, you can select the sauté function and let the chicken simmer for a few minutes until the sauce thickens.

8. Serve on buns, topped with coleslaw, if desired.

Honey Balsamic Chicken

This Honey Balsamic Chicken is so tender and flavor filled, your guest will think you've cooked for hours! This recipe was made to impress.

PREP 15 MIN | COOK 15 MIN | QUICK RELEASE

INGREDIENTS

3 chicken breasts

Kosher salt and freshly cracked black pepper

1 tablespoon olive or canola oil

1 large onion, thinly sliced

2 tomatoes, chopped

1/2 cup chicken broth

Chopped parsley, for garnish

For the sauce

1 1/2 teaspoons coriander seeds

1/4 star anise pod

Fresh cracked black pepper

1/4 cup balsamic vinegar

2 tablespoon honey

1 teaspoon crushed red pepper

1 teaspoon dried thyme

1 teaspoon dried oregano

INSTRUCTIONS

1. Wash and rinse the chicken with cold water. Pat dry with paper towels and season generously with salt and pepper.

2. Turn your Instant Pot on the Sauté mode. Once hot, add 1 tablespoon of oil and sear the chicken until all sides are nicely browned. Add onion and tomato and cook along with chicken until tomatoes start to break down – about 3 minutes.

3. In the meantime: In a small skillet, toast coriander seeds, anise pod, and black pepper until fragrant. Transfer to a spice grinder or mortar and allow to cool for a couple of minutes. Crush until coarsely ground.

4. To make the sauce, combine the balsamic vinegar, honey, oregano, thyme, and crushed red pepper in a small bowl. Add the ground spices and stir to mix well. Make sure the honey is completely dissolved. Set aside.

5. Pour in the chicken broth, then the sauce over chicken in the Instant Pot, give a quick stir and cover the lid. Select Pressure Cook at High pressure for 10 minutes.

6. Once done, release pressure. Sprinkle with the parsley and serve the honey balsamic chicken with the sauce on top of rice, pasta, or mashed potatoes.

THAI LEMONGRASS CHICKEN

This Lemongrass Chicken is tangy, the perfect combo of sweet and sour with hints of lemon and herbs. You can make it as spicy as you can handle. I'm pretty mild, so I don't stray from this recipe normally.

PREP 10 MIN | COOK 15 MIN | QUICK RELEASE

INGREDIENTS

- 13.5oz can full fat coconut milk
- 1 small yellow onion, quartered
- 4 Cloves garlic, smashed
- 1 inch piece fresh ginger
- 1 lemongrass stalk, roughly chopped
- 1 Tablespoon Thai red curry paste
- 2 Teaspoons fish sauce
- 2 Pounds boneless skinless chicken breasts
- 1 red bell pepper, chopped
- 1 jalapeño, seeds removed and chopped
- 1 cinnamon stick
- 1/4 Cup fresh cilantro, roughly chopped
- 1/4 Cup fresh basil, roughly torn
- juice of 1 lime
- Optional: peanuts, shredded carrots, and green onions for serving
- steamed rice for serving

INSTRUCTIONS

1. In a blender, combine the coconut milk, onion, garlic, ginger, lemongrass, curry paste, and fish sauce and blend until smooth.

2. In the bowl of your instant pot, combine the chicken, coconut sauce, bell pepper, jalapeño pepper, and cinnamon stick. Cover and cook on high pressure manual for 8 minutes.

3. Once done cooking, use the quick release function and release the steam. Remove and discard the cinnamon stick. Shred the chicken using two forks. Stir in the cilantro, basil, and lime juice.

4. Serve the chicken over rice and top with peanuts, carrots, and green onions, if desired.

Rotisserie Chicken

The BEST Rotisserie Chicken. This is my favorite way to cook a whole chicken. The pressure cooker locks in an intense amount of flavor and juice. The result is a texture much like a grocery store rotisserie chicken and one that you won't get by oven-roasting it. Recipe includes crispy skin and chicken gravy in 5 minutes!

PREP 10 MIN | COOK 40 MIN | NATURAL RELEASE

INGREDIENTS

1 Cup chicken broth

5 Pound whole chicken

2 Tablespoons olive oil

2 Teaspoons salt

1 Teaspoon black pepper

1 Tablespoon Greek Seasoning

2 1/2 Teaspoons paprika

1 Teaspoon garlic powder

1 Teaspoon onion powder

1/2 Tablespoon dried parsley

3 Tablespoons cornstarch

INSTRUCTIONS

1. Pour chicken broth into the pressure cooker.
2. In a small bowl, whisk together salt, black pepper, Greek seasoning, paprika, garlic powder, onion powder, and dried parsley. If your chicken is less than 5 pounds, still use this amount of seasoning but reduce salt by a little. In another small bowl, pour olive oil and set aside.
3. On a cutting board, place chicken. Reach into the neck cavity and rip off the neck. Check the middle cavity to ensure no other packaging is in the center.
4. Use a knife to loosen skin if needed. You should be able to fit fingers under the skin. Pour half the olive oil under skin. Sprinkle half the seasoning blend under the skin and evenly spread it throughout the underside of the skin. This will lock the flavor in.
5. Spread remaining oil on top of skin, Sprinkle evenly with remaining seasoning blend. Place chicken breast side up on trivet then place in the pressure cooker insert.
6. Secure lid. Turn value to Seal. Turn on pressure cooker. Press Pressure Cook and set it for 40 minutes on High Pressure. After the chicken has cooked, Allow pressure cooker to Natural Release.
7. Prepare a baking sheet with foil. Use 2 sets of kitchen tongs to lift trivet handles onto baking sheet. Place trivet with chicken in oven and Broil on for 5 minutes.
8. To make the gravy, set pressure cooker to Sauté mode. Whisk 3 tablespoons cornstarch into 3 tablespoons of cold water. Pour into pot. Allow to come to boil and whisk.
9. Carve chicken and serve with gravy.

Pork Recipes

Cooking is all about people. Food is maybe the only universal thing that really has the power to bring everyone together. No matter what culture, everywhere around the world, people get together to eat.

-*Guy Fieri*

Apple Pork Chops

These pressure cooker pork chops are rich and warm tasting with a hint of cinnamon and nutmeg in an incredible apple gravy.

PREP 5 MIN | COOK 5 MIN | NATURAL RELEASE

INGREDIENTS

3 apples, cored & sliced about 1/4" thick

1 Small sweet onion thinly sliced

2-4 pork chops

Salt & Pepper

1 Tablespoon vegetable oil

1 Cup + 1 Tablespoon Water (divided)

4 Tablespoon butter (unsalted)

4 Tablespoon brown sugar

1/4 tsp cinnamon

1/4 tsp nutmeg

Pinch of Salt

2 Tablespoon corn starch

3 Tablespoon cold water

INSTRUCTIONS

1. Season the pork chops with a sprinkling of salt and pepper on each side. Turn the pot to Sauté mode. When the display reads "Hot" add the oil to the pot.

2. Add the pork chops and brown on each side for about 4 minutes per side. Remove to a plate and set aside.

3. Add the onion and 1 Tablespoon water. Cook the onion, stirring frequently and scraping to deglaze the pot (get all of the brown bits off the bottom), with a wooden spoon.

4. When the onions are translucent and tender, add the butter and stir until melted. Add the apples and 1 cup water. Stir well.

5. Add the pork chops (and any juices on the plate) back in and just set them on top of the apples. Don't stir.

6. Put the lid on the pot and set the steam release valve to the Sealing position. Cancel the Sauté mode.

7. Select the Pressure Cook button add 10 (8 minutes for thinner chops) minutes. While the pork chops are cooking, mix together the brown sugar, cinnamon, nutmeg, and a pinch of salt.

8. When cooking is complete, let it naturally release pressure for 10 minutes. Remove the pork chops and turn the Sauté mode back on. Add the brown sugar mixture to the apple mixture in pot and stir.

9. Mix the corn starch with the cold water and stir the corn starch mix into the apple mixture, stirring constantly.

10. When the mixture thickens, turn off the pot. Remove apple gravy to a serving bowl immediately.

11. Serve the pork chops smothered in the warm apple gravy.

BRATS & BEER

*Making them is a time-honored football tradition, and
no tailgate party would be complete without them.*

PREP 5 MIN | COOK 6 MIN | NATURAL RELEASE

INGREDIENTS

2 T butter

7 Johnsonville Brats

1 bottle of beer

I use BASS Beer.

(*Michelob Ultra* is Best

if you're going low-carb)

INSTRUCTIONS

1. Turn on your instant pot and set to Sauté.
2. Brown the brats lightly in the butter on both sides, about 2-3 minutes each.
3. Remove all of the brats from the instant pot.
4. Place a rack on the bottom, set all of your bratwurst on top of the rack.
5. Carefully pour the beer over the bratwurst.
6. Set your instant pot to Pressure Cook and cook for 6 minutes.
7. Once done, do a Natural Release until the steam is released.
8. Remove brats and put on your favorite buns.

Spiral Honey Ham

This ham is just too good to save for the holidays. It makes a great weeknight meal and lots of leftover for sandwiches during the week.

PREP 10 MIN | COOK 30 MIN | NATURAL RELEASE

INGREDIENTS

6-7 lb. spiral ham bone in, fully cooked

2 cups apple cider or apple juice divided into two, ½ cup portions and one, 1-cup portion.

2 cups brown sugar divided into two 1-cup portions

¼ cup coarse ground mustard divided into two 2-tablespoon portions

¼ cup honey divided into two 2-tablespoon portions

Cooking / Non Stick Spray

INSTRUCTIONS

1. In a medium mixing bowl, whisk together ½ cup apple juice, 1 cup packed brown sugar, 2 tablespoons coarse ground mustard and 2 tablespoons honey.

2. Place the ham in a rimmed dish and pour the apple juice mixture over the entire ham. Rub it in and around the ham – being sure to get in-between the slices of ham (as much as possible).

3. Spray the Instant Pot pan insert with cooking spray and pour 1 cup apple juice in the bottom. Place the ham in the Instant Pot and pour any leftover juices that had drained off the ham back over the ham. Cover and lock the lid in place with the vent closed. Set the Instant Pot on Pressure Cook at High Pressure for 15 minutes. Allow the steam to release naturally. While the ham is cooking, cover a rimmed baking sheet with foil, and spray the foil with nonstick spray.

4. Set the oven to broil.

5. Remove the ham from the pressure cooker and place it on the prepared baking sheet.

6. Combine ½ cup apple juice, 2 tablespoons coarse mustard and 2 tablespoons honey in a small bowl. Brush the apple juice mixture over the cooked ham. Rub (and press) 1-cup brown sugar into the top surfaces of the ham, and place the ham under the broiler 5-10 minutes or until the glaze is bubbly and caramelized

7. Transfer the ham to a cooling rack and cool for a few minutes. Serve warm or cold. It is delicious either way.

Honey Mustard Pork Chops

Pork chops are a great economical cut and cook up quickly, making them ideal for busy weeknight meals.

PREP 10 MIN | COOK 20 MIN | NATURAL RELEASE

INGREDIENTS

1 Tablespoon Olive Oil

4 Boneless Pork Chops

1 Onion, chopped

1 cup Water

3 Tablespoons Whole Grain Mustard

1 Tablespoon Prepared Mustard

2 Tablespoons Honey

Salt and Pepper, to taste

1 sprig Rosemary

1 teaspoon Cornstarch, + 1 tablespoon cold water, mixed

INSTRUCTIONS

1. Set instant pot to sauté. Add olive oil and add pork chops to inner pot.

2. Sprinkle with salt and pepper and brown on both sides.

3. Add the onion and continue cooking for 1 minute.

4. Mix water, both mustards, honey, salt and pepper in a measuring jug.

5. Switch off the instant pot and pour the water mix over the pork chops.

6. Scrape the browned bits off the bottom, then add the rosemary.

7. Close the instant pot and turn the valve to sealing. Select Pressure Cook on high pressure for 8 minutes.

8. Switch off the instant pot and do a natural pressure release for 5 minutes, then quick release any remaining pressure before opening the lid.

9. Remove pork chops from the pot.

10. To thicken the sauce, stir in the cornstarch mix into the pot and stir.

11. Set the pot to sauté and cook, stirring, for about a minute or until sauce has thickened.

12. Serve over pork chops.

BBQ Pulled Pork

This is a good recipe if you arrive home before everyone else and happen to have a little extra time. Great for leftovers too!

PREP 15 MIN | COOK 60 MIN | NATURAL RELEASE

INGREDIENTS

- **3-4 pound pork roast**
- **3 Tablespoons smoked paprika**
- **1 Tablespoon salt**
- **1 Tablespoon pepper**
- **1 teaspoon garlic powder**
- **1/3 cup liquid smoke**
- **2 cups barbecue sauce, any variety**
- **½ cup water**

INSTRUCTIONS

1. Add pork roast to bottom of Instant Pot, then add paprika, salt, pepper, garlic powder, liquid smoke, barbeque sauce, and water.
2. Twist lid on and turn valve to sealing.
3. Select Pressure Cook at High Pressure for 60 minutes.
4. Let Natural release for at least 10 minutes, then Quick Release any remaining pressure.
5. If pork is too tough to shred, replace lid and cook another 3 minutes.
6. Pick roast up with forks, shred, and serve on buns.

Pork Adobo

Try this melt in your mouth Pork Adobo Recipe using a perfect balance of saltiness, acidity, and garlicky goodness.

PREP 10 MIN | COOK 35 MIN | QUICK RELEASE

INGREDIENTS

1 Tablespoon canola oil

3 Pounds pork butt, cut into 1 1/2-inch cubes

salt and pepper to taste

1 onion, peeled and sliced thinly

6 cloves garlic, peeled and crushed

1/2 Teaspoon peppercorns

2 bay leaves

1/4 Cup vinegar

1/4 Cup soy sauce

1/4 Cup water

INSTRUCTIONS

1. Using the sauté function, heat oil. Add pork cubes and cook, turning as needed, until browned on all sides. Season with salt and pepper to taste.

2. Add onions, garlic, peppercorns, and bay leaves.

3. In a bowl, combine vinegar, soy sauce, and water. Pour into the pot over meat mixture.

4. Close the lid making sure the valve is on SEALING position and cook on HIGH pressure for 10 minutes. Do a quick release and open lid.

5. Turn back to sauté feature and simmer for about 15 to 20 minutes or until sauce is thickened.

6. Add more salt and pepper as needed. Serve hot with steamed rice or pasta.

Pork BBQ Baby Back Ribs

Fall-off-the-bone ribs that will have you licking your fingers in no time.

PREP 10 MIN | COOK 35 MIN | QUICK RELEASE

INGREDIENTS

4 Pounds baby back pork ribs, membrane removed

3 Tablespoons brown sugar

3 Teaspoons sea salt

2 Teaspoons garlic powder

2 Teaspoons smoked paprika

1 Teaspoon ground black pepper

1 Cup apple cider vinegar

1 Cup water

INSTRUCTIONS

1. Add the brown sugar, sea salt, garlic powder, smoked paprika and pepper to a small bowl, and stir to combine.

2. Remove membrane from back of ribs, and rub seasoning mix over ribs.

3. Add water and apple cider vinegar to Instant Pot, and place trivet on bottom of pot.

4. Place seasoned ribs on trivet, cover, move valve to sealing position, and hit Pressure Cook for 20 minutes.

5. Allow to naturally release for 10 minutes, then move valve to quick release until pin drops.

6. Open lid, remove ribs to foil lined baking sheet, and brush barbecue sauce over ribs.

7. Place ribs in oven, and broil for 5 minutes or until ribs bubble and look crisp.

8. Remove ribs from oven, cut, and enjoy!

Pork Chile Verde

Pork Chile Verde is a Keto and Paleo friendly recipe using chicken thighs, tomatillos, and chile peppers.

PREP 15 MIN | COOK 25 MIN | NATURAL RELEASE

INGREDIENTS

2 Pounds boneless skinless chicken thighs

12oz tomatillos quartered

8oz poblano peppers

4oz jalapeño pepper

1/2 onion, chopped

1/4 Cup water

5 Cloves garlic

2 Teaspoons ground cumin

1 1/2 Teaspoons salt

INSTRUCTIONS

1. Add tomatillos, poblanos, jalapeños, onions, and water to the pressure cooker. Sprinkle garlic, cumin, and salt on top evenly. Lastly, add chicken thighs.

2. Secure and seal the lid. Select Pressure Cook Button. Cook at high pressure for 15 minutes, followed by a Natural Pressure release.

3. Uncover and remove the chicken to a cutting board. Cut into bite-sized pieces. Set aside.

4. Add cilantro and lime juice to the pressure cooker. Use an immersion blender or countertop blender to puree the mixture.

5. Select the sauté mode on the pressure cooker. Return the chicken to the mixture and add back to pot. Boil for about 10 minutes to thicken the sauce, stirring occasionally. Serve and garnish with additional cilantro.

Pork Pot Roast

If you're looking for a delicious easy and flavorful pork roast and potatoes recipe, I've got just the recipe for you! This recipes comes together in a flash and the whole family will be singing your praises in no time.

PREP 25 MIN | COOK 75 MIN | NATURAL RELEASE

INGREDIENTS

2 Tablespoons brown sugar

1/2 Tablespoon garlic powder

1 Teaspoon onion powder

1.5 Teaspoons coarse salt

1/2 Teaspoon cinnamon

1 Teaspoon dried thyme

1/2 Teaspoon pepper

2 pound pork shoulder roast

1/4 Cup olive oil, divided

2 cloves garlic, minced

1/2 yellow onion, chopped

1/2 Cup dry red wine (cabernet or pinot noir)

1 Cup broth (any kind)

2 sprigs fresh rosemary

2 large carrots, chopped into 1.5-inch chunks

2 large potatoes, chopped into chunks

1/4 – 1/2 Cup balsamic vinegar

2 Tablespoons corn starch

INSTRUCTIONS

1. First, mix together all dry rub spices in a bowl using a fork to smooth.
2. Next, rub the spice mixture all over your pork roast with your hands. Be sure that every inch of the roast is covered. Set aside.
3. Turn on the sauté feature of your pot and add two tablespoons of olive oil to the pot.
4. When olive is warm add onions and garlic. Cook for 2-3 minutes and remove from pot.
5. Add the last two tablespoons of olive oil to the pot and when olive oil is warm add pork roast and sear for 2-3 minutes on each side to brown the pork.
6. Remove pork from pot and deglaze your pot by pouring wine and broth into the bottom. Scrape all of the brown bits from the bottom with a wooden spoon. Then, add cooked onion and garlic, and fresh rosemary to the liquid and place on lid.
7. Finally, place pork roast on top of the trivet and cover pot. Seal and set it to Pressure Cook at high pressure for 70 minutes.
8. Quick release pressure and add carrots and potatoes to Instant Pot. Cover again and set pot to Pressure Cook at high pressure for 3 additional minutes. Quick release again and remove pork roast and veggies from the pot and place them in a large bowl. Throw rosemary sprigs away.
9. Remove trivet and set aside. Add balsamic vinegar to the wine sauce. Mix well and then sprinkle in corn starch to the wine sauce.
10. Turn sauté feature on and whisk mixture until the corn starch has dissolved. Cook for 3-4 minutes or until sauce thickens Place veggies and pork roast back into the Instant Pot, stir well and serve.

Pork Chops with Creamy Ranch Gravy

Deliciously tender pork chops cooked in the Instant Pot and smothered with a creamy ranch gravy. This is one of the recipes that everyone in my house will eat without complaints.

PREP 5 MIN | COOK 20 MIN | NATURAL RELEASE

INGREDIENTS

5 Pork Chops

1 Tablespoon Olive Oil

1 Teaspoon Salt

1/2 Teaspoon Garlic Powder

1/2 Teaspoon Pepper

1 Envelope Ranch Dressing Mix

1 One Ounce Envelope Brown Gravy Mix

1 10.5 Ounce Can Cream of Mushroom Soup

2 Cups Beef Broth

2 Tablespoons Cornstarch

2 Tablespoons Water

INSTRUCTIONS

1. Season the pork chops on both sides with the salt, garlic powder, and pepper.

2. Add the olive oil to the instant pot and turn on to sauté. When the oil is hot, brown the pork chops on each side for 2-3 minutes just until browned.

3. Remove the pork chops from the instant pot.

4. Pour 1/4 cup of the beef broth (this doesn't have to be exact) into the instant pot and use a wooden spoon to deglaze the bottom of the pot.

5. Turn the instant pot off and add the pork chops along with the ranch dressing mix, brown gravy mix, cream of mushroom soup, and remaining beef broth to the pot. (I put the chops in last)

6. Place the lid on the pot and set the valve to sealing. Cook on Pressure Cook for 8 minutes. When cooking complete, Natural Release the pressure.

7. After 10 minutes of natural pressure release, release any remaining pressure from the pot and remove the lid.

8. Remove the pork chops from the pot to a serving plate.

9. In a small bowl whisk together the cornstarch and water. Turn the instant pot on to sauté and whisk in the cornstarch mixture. Whisk constantly until gravy is thick, then, turn off the instant pot.

10. Serve the pork chops with the gravy and your favorite side dishes.

Sweet Balsamic Pork Loin

We love anything with a sweet sauce like this Sweet Balsamic Pork. It is tender moist and covered in a sweet brown sugar balsamic sauce.

PREP 10 MIN | COOK 35 MIN | QUICK RELEASE

INGREDIENTS

1 tablespoon olive oil

2-3 pound pork roast

Salt & pepper

Sauce

3 cloves garlic pressed with a garlic press

1/4 cup brown sugar

1/4 cup balsamic vinegar

1/4 cup water

1 tablespoon cornstarch

1 tablespoon soy sauce

1 tablespoon rosemary chopped

INSTRUCTIONS

1. Mix all sauce ingredients in a small bowl.
2. Heat the Instant Pot on Sauté function. Pour in the oil.
3. Season the pork on both sides with salt and pepper. Brown on all sides.
4. Turn off the sauté mode and add the sauce to the pork in the pot. Turn to Pressure Cook, seal lid and cook at High Pressure for 35 minutes.
5. When cooking is complete, turn pot off and let the pressure naturally release.
6. Slice and serve with plenty of sauce.

Thai Moo Wan Sweet Pork

This is a very popular dish in Thai Restaurants. It is sweet and filling.

PREP 5 MIN | COOK 15 MIN | NATURAL RELEASE

INGREDIENTS

2 Tablespoons Vegetable Oil

3 large Shallots sliced medium thick

3 Tablespoons Soy Sauce

3 cloves Fresh Garlic minced

1/4 cup Light Brown Sugar divided

1/4 cup Palm Sugar divided

2 Tablespoons Sweet/Black Soy Sauce

2 Tablespoons Fish Sauce

1 teaspoon Sambal Oelek Ground Chili Paste

1/4 teaspoon Ground Pepper

2 pounds Pork Shoulder cut into 1/4" x 2" strips

Scallions for garnish

Caramelized & Crispy Onions for garnish

INSTRUCTIONS

1. Select the Sauté or browning button on your Pressure Cooker and allow to fully heat.

2. Add Oil and Shallots to cooking pot and Sauté for two minutes. Add Garlic and Sauté another 30 seconds.

3. Add Soy Sauce, Fish Sauce, Sambal Oelek, White Pepper and half the Sugars to cooking pot and let simmer for 3 minutes. Turn off Pressure Cooker.

4. Add Pork and combine with the Sauce.

5. Lock on lid and close valve. Select Pressure Cook at High Pressure for 6 minutes. When cooking completed, wait 10 minutes and then release the rest of the pressure.

6. Remove lid, Mix in the rest of the Sugar. Select Sauté and let simmer until Sauce has thickened and can be parted with a spatula.

7. Garnish with crispy caramelized Onions and Scallions. Serve with a green salad with an acidic dressing, like Balsamic Vinegar.

Seafood Recipes

I'm on a seafood diet - I see food, I eat it.

-Dolly Parton

Cajun Shrimp & Grits

I'd have to turn in my Southern card if I didn't include a Shrimp & Grits recipe.

PREP 15 MIN | COOK 25 MIN | Sauté Only

INGREDIENTS

4 Cups of water

2 Cloves garlic, minced

Salt & Pepper to Taste

¾ Cup Grits, stone ground (not instant)

2 Tablespoons of Land O'Lakes whipped butter

4 Slices of cooked bacon, chopped

1.5 Pounds of Large Cooked Shrimp (Peeled)

2 Roma tomatoes, chopped

3 Teaspoons Cajun seasoning

4 Teaspoons fresh lemon juice

Minced Jalapeño, Optional

INSTRUCTIONS

1. Select the sauté setting on your Instant Pot. Adjust time for high heat (30 minutes). Add water, garlic, salt & pepper and bring to a boil.

2. Add the grits ¼ cup at a time while stirring constantly after each addition.

3. Select sauté setting, reduce heat to low (5 minutes) and cook grits for 15 minutes, stirring quite a few times.

4. Stir in whipped butter and cooked bacon.

5. After butter melts, add all remaining ingredients. Cook for 10 more minutes or until heated through.

6. Serve immediately and garnish with jalapeño if desired.

Creamy Herb Parmesan Salmon

Perfect quick weeknight and elegant meal. For those nights when the boss is coming to dinner with no notice. It will seem as you've cooked all day.

PREP 15 MIN | COOK 20 MIN | QUICK RELEASE

INGREDIENTS

1/2 Cup water

1.5 Teaspoon minced garlic

4 frozen salmon filets

1/2 Cup heavy cream

1 Cup parmesan cheese grated

1 Tablespoon chopped fresh chives

1 Tablespoon chopped fresh parsley

1 Tablespoon fresh dill

1 Teaspoon fresh lemon juice

Salt and pepper to taste

INSTRUCTIONS

1. Place water and garlic in insert with trivet on top. Place salmon on top of trivet.

2. Close pressure cooker and set on Pressure Cook at High Pressure for 4-5 minutes. (Depending on your doneness preference)

3. Once timer goes off, quick release the pressure. Remove salmon and trivet from the pot.

4. Turn off pressure cooker and set to Sauté and adjust to Normal.

5. Once water begins to boil, whisk in the heavy cream and bring to a boil again. Allow to boil for about 2-3 minutes. The mixture should be able to stick to the back of a spoon.

6. Turn off pressure cooker and remove insert from pot. Whisk in chives, parsley, dill, parmesan cheese, and lemon juice. Salt and pepper to taste.

Drunken Clams

Heyyyyy Bartender...

PREP 10 MIN | COOK 5 MIN | QUICK RELEASE

INGREDIENTS

3 Pounds clams, Fresh, frozen or canned

1/2 stick butter

3 Tablespoons olive oil

6 cloves garlic, chopped

1/2 cup white wine

2 cups of chicken broth

2 8oz cans chopped clams

1 cup grape or cherry tomatoes cut in half

Fresh chopped parsley

INSTRUCTIONS

1. Place clams in a bowl with cold wate and let soak to remove any sand.

2. Select Sauté Function and Butter. Once butter is melted, add olive oil and garlic. Sauté for 1 minute until garlic infuses the butter and oil mixture.

3. Add white wine and sauté about 1 minute to deglaze the pot.

4. Add clams, with juice if using canned, and chicken broth.

5. Secure the lid and Select Pressure Cook at High Pressure for 1 minute. When cooking is complete, Quick Release pressure.

6. Serve and top with fresh chopped parsley. Great with a crusty bread for dipping.

Indian Curry Fish

Indian Curry Fish is inspired by a popular fish curry that's traditional in the Southern part of India. This mild coconut milk-based curry with a tinge of tartness is so quick and easy to make. Kick up the heat by adding more jalapeño. Serve over rice.

PREP 5 MIN | COOK 10 MIN | QUICK RELEASE

INGREDIENTS

- 2 Tablespoons coconut oil
- 10 curry leaves
- 1 cup onion chopped
- 1 Tablespoon garlic
- 1 Tablespoon ginger
- 1/2 jalapeño pepper sliced
- 1 cup tomato chopped
- 1 teaspoon ground coriander
- 1/4 teaspoon ground cumin
- 1/2 teaspoon turmeric
- 1/2 teaspoon black pepper
- 1 teaspoon salt
- 2 Tablespoons water
- 1 cup canned coconut milk
- 1 1/2 Pounds cod fillets (cut in chunks)
- 1 Teaspoon lime juice
- Fresh cilantro leaves for garnish optional
- Fresh tomato slices for garnish optional

INSTRUCTIONS

1. Select the Sauté function and pre-heat the Instant Pot.
2. Add coconut oil to the pre-heated inner pot and allow it to heat up.
3. Add curry leaves and stir for about 20 seconds.
4. Add onions, garlic, ginger and jalapeño to the pot. Stir until onions are translucent.
5. Add tomatoes and sauté until the tomatoes release their liquid and start breaking down. Add in coriander, cumin, turmeric, black pepper, and salt. Sauté until spices are fragrant, about 30 seconds. Be careful not to burn!
6. Deglaze pot with water about 1 minute. Stir in coconut milk, and carefully add in fish pieces.
7. Make sure the sauce coasts the entire fish, Close the lid and pressure cook for 2 minutes at high pressure.
8. Quick Release pressure and open the lid.
9. Add lime juice and gently stir the curry without breaking up the fish.
10. Carefully remove fish and gravy into a serving bowl. Garnish with chopped cilantro and fresh tomato slices.

Lobster Rolls

Lobster rolls are a staple summer meal throughout the Maritime Provinces in Canada, particularly Nova Scotia where they may also appear on hamburger buns, baguettes, or other types of bread rolls and even pita pockets. The traditional sides are potato chips and dill pickles.

PREP 5 MIN | COOK 3 MIN | QUICK RELEASE

INGREDIENTS

- 1 ½ Cups water
- 4 lobster tails (4 - 5 oz. thawed or fresh)
- 2 Tablespoons mayonnaise
- ½ Teaspoon Kosher salt
- ¼ Teaspoon black pepper
- ¼ Cup celery, minced
- 2 green onions, tender green parts only, sliced thinly
- 4 French rolls
- 2 Tablespoons Unsalted butter, room temperature

INSTRUCTIONS

1. Pour water in the Instant Pot. Add steamer rack.
2. Using kitchen shears, cut open top side of lobster along its length. Gently pull top meat out of shell. Arrange in a single layer on steamer rack.
3. Put lid on Instant Pot and turn value to sealing. Select Pressure Cook for 3 minutes at LOW pressure.
4. Prepare an ice bath.
5. Quick Release and move lobster tails to ice bath for 5 minutes.
6. Pull meat out of tails and pat dry with a paper towel. Cut into ½ inch pieces.
7. In a bowl, mix lobster, mayonnaise, salt, pepper, celery and green onions.
8. Spread butter on French rolls and toast on skillet until golden brown.
9. Spoon lobster mixture onto rolls and serve immediately.

Low Country Boil

We love spreading this out all around the table with friends and the room becomes filled with conversation and laughter. It is our end of the summer tradition, and crab legs (just put in shell and all) can be substituted for shrimp to change it up.

PREP 10 MIN | COOK 10 MIN | QUICK RELEASE

INGREDIENTS

1 1/2 pounds baby red potatoes

1 package of Polish Kielbasa, cut in 1 inch pieces

1/2 medium sweet onion, chopped

4 teaspoons Old Bay seasoning, divided

1 tablespoon hot sauce

3 ears corn, halved

1 (16-ounce) pilsner or lager beer

1 1/2 pounds medium shrimp, shell-on

1/4 cup unsalted butter

3 cloves garlic, minced

2 tablespoons chopped fresh parsley leaves

1 lemon, cut into wedges

INSTRUCTIONS

1. Place potatoes, sausage, onion, 3 teaspoons Old Bay seasoning and hot sauce into Instant Pot. Stir until well until combined. Top with corn and beer.

2. Select Pressure Cook setting; adjust pressure to high, and set time for 5 minutes. When finished cooking, quick-release pressure.

3. Add shrimp. Select Pressure Cook; adjust pressure to high, and set time for 1 minute. When finished cooking, quick-release pressure.

4. Melt butter in a small skillet over medium low heat. Stir in garlic and remaining 1 teaspoon Old Bay seasoning until fragrant, about 1-2 minutes.

5. Serve shrimp mixture immediately, drizzled with butter mixture, garnished with parsley and lemon, if desired.

Saipan Shrimp

Such a great meal, you might not want to leave it unattended in the office refrigerator.

PREP 10 MIN | COOK 5 MIN | QUICK RELEASE

INGREDIENTS

4 Tablespoons butter

1 onion chopped

4 Cloves garlic, chopped

1 Teaspoon paprika

1 Teaspoon turmeric

1/2 Teaspoon salt

1/4 Teaspoon black pepper

1/4 Teaspoon red pepper flakes

1 Red bell pepper, chopped

1 Cup Jasmine rice, uncooked

1 Cup chicken broth

1/2 Cup white wine

1 Pound frozen jumbo shrimp, uncooked and peeled

1/4 Cup cilantro optional

INSTRUCTIONS

1. Set Instant Pot to Sauté function. Add butter to pot and melt. Add onions and cook until softened. Add garlic and cook for about a minute more.

2. Add paprika, turmeric, salt, black pepper, and red pepper flakes. Stir and cook for about 1 minute. Add red bell peppers.

3. Add rice and stir. Cook for about 30 seconds to 1 minute. Add chicken broth and white wine. Deglaze your pot by stirring to ensure that there is no food stuck to the bottom of the pot.

4. Add shrimp on top. Turn off Instant Pot and cover. Make sure valve is set to sealing.

5. Set Instant Pot to Pressure Cook at High Pressure for 5 minutes. When done, quick release.

6. Remove from pot and top with Cilantro.

Shrimp Fettuccine Alfredo

Shrimp Fettuccine Alfredo is one of life's greatest comfort foods. It's creamy, cheesy, carb-y, and extremely flavorful.

PREP 5 MIN | COOK 20 MIN | NATURAL RELEASE

INGREDIENTS

1 Pound large shrimp

4 Cups chicken broth

2 Tablespoons garlic minced

1/4 Teaspoon ground nutmeg

1 Teaspoon sea salt

16oz fettuccine broken in half

2 Cups heavy cream

6oz Parmigiano-Reggiano cheese grated

INSTRUCTIONS

1. Defrost shrimp (if frozen) in cold water. Remove shells and tails.

2. Add chicken broth, garlic, nutmeg, and salt to pot and mix well.

3. Then add fettuccine noodles, making sure to spread them apart as much as possible. DO NOT STIR! (Noodles will break)

4. Then add cream, making sure that all noodles are submerged. DO NOT STIR!

5. Lock lid and cook for 2 minutes at high pressure using the Pressure Cooker button. Once cook time is complete, allow pressure to release naturally for 5 minutes. Then quick-release remaining pressure. (If starchy bubbles try to escape the vent, simply close the vent for 30 seconds or so, then release again in intervals.)

6. Meanwhile, grate Parmigiano-Reggiano cheese.

7. Mix pasta and sauce well, making sure to break up any noodles that may be stuck together. Add all cheese to the pot and mix well.

8. Finally, add shrimp to pot and mix, making sure to submerge all shrimp. Return lid to pot and let sit for about 10 minutes. The shrimp will cook in the residual heat, and the sauce will thicken the longer it sits.

9. Serve topped with cracked black pepper and a sprinkle of cheese.

Shrimp Scampi

Shrimp scampi is succulent seafood and tomatoes mixed in a tangy lemon garlic butter sauce which pairs nicely with angel hair pasta.

PREP 5 MIN | COOK 15 MIN | QUICK RELEASE

INGREDIENTS

2 Tablespoons butter

1 Tablespoon olive oil

2 whole shallots, minced

1/4 cup white wine

2 lb. peeled shrimp

16 oz. angel hair pasta, broken in half

2 cups chicken stock

1/2 whole fresh lemon

1 pinch sea salt and pepper, to taste

1/4 tsp red pepper flakes

1 Tablespoon fresh parsley

Parmesan cheese for garnish

INSTRUCTIONS

1. Turn the instant pot on sauté mode. Melt butter, add oil and shallots. Sauté for 2-3 minutes until fragrant.

2. Add wine and cook until reduced about 3 minutes.

3. Add shrimp, season with salt, pepper and pepper flakes. Sprinkle with fresh lemon and continue to sauté until shrimp is well coated.

4. Remove shrimp from pot and add in chicken stock and pasta. Separate the pasta the best you can. Top with shrimp and cover the pot. Cancel sauté mode and select pressure cook on high for 3 minutes.

5. When done, Natural Release 5 minutes then quick release remaining pressure. Remove contents to a serving dish.

6. Season with fresh parsley and serve with parmesan cheese.

Steamed Alaskan Crab

My favorite meal ever. I could eat these every day. You know what's the absolute BEST about this recipe? NO more waiting, fighting, or being frustrated at buffets trying to get maybe one or two legs. You can have as many as you want at your own table.

PREP 5 MIN | COOK 2 MIN | QUICK RELEASE

INGREDIENTS

2 Pounds frozen crab legs

1 Cup water

1 bag of Zatarains Seafood Spices

4 Tablespoons butter, melted

Lemon juice

INSTRUCTIONS

1. Put the steamer basket into the Instant Pot and place in crab legs.

2. Pour in water, add spice bag and seal the lid. Turn valve to sealing.

3. Select Pressure Cook at High pressure for 2 minutes. and quick release pressure when complete.

4. Crab legs should be bright pink.

5. Mix lemon juice with melted butter and serve.

Teriyaki Salmon

This recipe is always a hit. Leftovers are amazing on a salad!

PREP 10 MIN | COOK 10 MIN | QUICK RELEASE

INGREDIENTS

1/2 cup soy sauce

1/4 cup mirin sweet rice wine

1/2 cup chicken broth

1 tsp sesame oil

2 garlic cloves minced

2 tsp fresh ginger grated, or finely chopped

1 cup water

1 to 1.5 lbs. fresh salmon filets

Freshly ground black pepper

1 teaspoon cornstarch mixed with 1 tablespoon water

4 scallions thinly sliced, for garnish

2 Tablespoons sesame seeds for garnish

INSTRUCTIONS

1. In a medium bowl, mix together the soy sauce, mirin, broth, sesame oil, garlic and ginger.

2. Season the salmon with the pepper.

3. Place the salmon in a 7-inch spring form pan lined with foil, or small loaf pans, or a sturdy aluminum foil packet, then loosely sealed. (I use the foil packets)

4. Pour 1/3 cup of the marinade over the salmon and place in the fridge for 15 minutes.

5. Add 1 cup water into the Instant Pot and lower in the steam trivet.

6. Lower the vessel with marinated salmon onto the steam trivet. Lock the lid into place and select Pressure Cook on the High Pressure for 6 minutes.

7. After cooking, Quick Release the pressure. Unlock and remove the lid.

8. While the fish is cooking, add the remaining marinade into a small pan and bring to a boil. Add the cornstarch mixture, and whisk until slightly thickened and glossy.

9. Carefully remove the steamer trivet from the pot and with a large slotted spatula, transfer the fish to a plate

10. Pour a couple tablespoons of the reduced teriyaki sauce over the fillets.

11. Garnish with sliced scallions and sesame seeds. Put remaining sauce on table.

Tuscan Shrimp

A fantastic taste of Tuscany. Make this yummy dinner a vacation.

PREP 10 MIN | COOK 20 MIN | QUICK RELEASE

INGREDIENTS

32oz chicken broth

1/2 Cup oil packed sun dried tomatoes with herbs, drained and dab excess oil off with paper towels, chopped

2 Teaspoons Italian seasoning

1 Tablespoon minced garlic

Salt and freshly ground black pepper

2 Pounds frozen peeled shrimp

12oz uncooked pasta

5oz fresh baby spinach

8oz Package cream cheese, cut into cubes and softened

1 Cup finely shredded parmesan cheese

1/4 Cup chopped fresh basil

INSTRUCTIONS

1. In an Instant Pot stir together broth, tomatoes, Italian seasoning, garlic, 1/4 tsp salt and 1/4 tsp pepper.

2. Stir in shrimp and pasta (and try to submerge down into broth).

3. Secure the lid in place, then turn the valve is to sealing. Select the Pressure Cook setting on high pressure for 4 minutes.

4. Quick Release, when cooking completed. Immediately stir noodles to separate. Add in spinach, cream cheese and parmesan.

5. Toss well. Let rest for about 5 - 10 minutes to thicken (it will be soupy at first, but as it cools it will thicken).

6. Toss in basil just before serving.

Bean & Legume Recipes

The things I learned sitting on the porch shelling peas or snapping green beans, can never be taught in any school classroom. Share this time with your kids, get to know them, it can teach everyone some valuable lessons.

-Bitsy Keown

Instant Pot Dry Bean Basics

Rinse and sort your dried beans, check them over for rocks or debris.

Dry beans do not have to be soaked, but are better for digestion if soaked overnight. If soaking overnight is not an option in your busy schedule, after cooking the beans add a small splash of apple cider vinegar to them. It will help aid with digestion of the beans.

- **4 cups liquid to 1 pound of beans:** Best for beans that you don't plan on straining, like the pinto bean side dishes you get at Mexican restaurants. Less water means a flavorful, thicker, and more starchy sauce
- **5 cups liquid to 1 pound of beans:** Best for beans that you want to be less starchy and infused with flavor even after straining some of the extra liquid. This is perfect for Mexican food fillings, salads, salsas, and refried beans
- **6 cups liquid to 1 pound of beans:** Best for beans that are hardly starchy and only mildly seasoned. These are perfect for bagging and freezing.

Cook on high pressure for directed time.

Once cook time has released, let pressure release naturally for at least 20 minutes before trying to do a quick release of pressure.

Once beans have finished cooking, add in a splash of apple cider vinegar (if needed) and salt.

Dried Beans, Legumes, and Lentils	Dry Cook Time (Minutes)	Soaked Cook Time (Minutes)
Black Beans	20 - 25	6 - 8
Black-eye Peas	14 - 18	4 - 5
Chickpeas	35 - 40	10 - 15
Cannellini Beans	30 - 35	6 - 9
Great Northern Beans	25 - 30	7 - 8
Kidney Beans, Red	15 - 20	7 - 8
Lentils, Green	8 - 10	n/a
Lentils, Brown	8 - 10	n/a
Lentils, Red, Split	1 - 2	n/a
Lentils, Yellow, Split	1 - 2	n/a
Lima Beans	12 - 14	6 - 10
Navy Beans	20 - 25	7 - 8
Pinto Beans	25 - 30	6 - 9
Peas	16 - 20	10 - 12
Soy Beans	35 - 45	18 - 20

Black Beans

A small black variety of the kidney bean, having cream-colored flesh and a sweet flavor, used in southern and Latin-American cuisine.

PREP 5 MIN | COOK 45 MIN | NATURAL RELEASE

INGREDIENTS

2 Tablespoons olive oil

6 cloves of garlic, minced

1 large green bell pepper, diced

1 large yellow onion, diced

2 Teaspoons salt

1 Teaspoon black pepper

1/2 Teaspoon cumin

1/2 Teaspoon cayenne pepper

1 Pound dry black beans

6 Cups chicken broth

Garnish with cilantro

INSTRUCTIONS

1. Turn on the Instant Pot to Sauté setting and pour the oil into pot. Sauté the garlic, pepper, and onion until soft;
2. 3-5 minutes.
3. Push the garlic, pepper and onion to the side, make a clear space in the pot to toast the spices. Add the salt, pepper, cumin, Cayenne; toast for 1 minute. Turn the Instant Pot off.
4. Add the dried beans and the chicken broth.
5. Place the lid on the pot and lock. Turn value to sealing. Select Pressure Cook at High Pressure for 45 minutes.
6. Once cooking completed, let it Naturally Release. Open pot and stir beans.
7. Garnish with cilantro prior to serving.

Cheesy Southwestern Lentils & Brown Rice

Southwestern Lentil and Brown Rice Bake is a cheesy, delicious meatless comfort food even a carnivore will love and is super easy to prepare.

PREP 10 MIN | COOK 15 MIN | NATURAL RELEASE

INGREDIENTS

1/2 red onion finely chopped

1/2 red bell pepper finely chopped

4 cloves garlic,

3/4 Cup Bob's Red Mill brown rice

3/4 Cup Bob's Red Mill brown lentils

2 1/2 Cups vegetable broth

1 Can petite diced tomatoes 15 oz

1 Can diced green chilies 4 oz

1 Tablespoon taco seasoning

2 Teaspoons dried oregano

1 Teaspoon kosher salt

1/2 Teaspoon Black pepper

2 Cups shredded cheddar cheese

1/4 Cup chopped fresh cilantro for topping

INSTRUCTIONS

1. Add all ingredients, except cheese and cilantro, to your Instant Pot. Select Pressure Cook at High Pressure for 15 minutes.

2. Allow pressure to naturally release for 15 minutes then release remaining pressure.

3. Remove cover and stir in 1 Cup of the cheese. Sprinkle remaining 1 Cup of cheese over the top and replace the cover. Allow to stand for 5 minutes.

4. Sprinkle with cilantro and serve.

Chickpea Masala

Quick recipe that is a good side for Chicken Tikka Masala.

PREP 15 MIN | COOK 15 MIN | QUICK RELEASE

INGREDIENTS

1 Tablespoon coconut oil

2 yellow onions, diced

4 cloves garlic, minced

2 Cans chickpeas

1 Tablespoon chili powder

1 Tablespoon Garam Masala

2 Teaspoon cumin

1 Teaspoon turmeric

1 Teaspoon salt

1 Can, 14.5oz, diced tomatoes

1 Can, 14.5oz, crushed tomatoes

1 Tablespoon lemon juice

3 Cups fresh baby spinach, chopped

Cilantro for garnish (optional)

INSTRUCTIONS

1. Add the following ingredients to the Instant Pot in this order: coconut oil, onions, garlic, chickpeas, chili powder, garam masala, cumin, turmeric, salt, diced tomatoes and crushed tomatoes. Place the lid on Instant Pot, make sure valve is set to sealing.

2. Select the Pressure Cook button at High Pressure for 2 minutes.

3. Perform a quick release, then open lid when pressure button has dropped and lid opens easily. Stir in lemon juice and baby spinach. Serve over rice and garnish with cilantro.

Cowboy Beans

Cowboy beans are perfect for a big cookout, tailgating, or an everyday family meal. Lean ground beef makes this a hearty meal on its own, or you might want to serve this as a side dish.

PREP 15 MIN | COOK 25 MIN | NATURAL RELEASE

INGREDIENTS

1 1/2 Pounds ground beef

1/2 Pound thick cut bacon, chopped (4-6 slices)

1 large onion, diced

6 cloves garlic, pressed or minced

2/3 Cup water

1 Pound Kielbasa sausage, smoked (cut into 1 1/2" pieces)

2 Cans, 28oz, pork & beans

1/2 Cup ketchup

1 Can, 14oz, red kidney beans, drained & rinsed

1/2 Cup barbecue sauce

1 1/2 Tablespoon Dijon mustard

1/3 Cup molasses

1/2 Teaspoon black pepper

1 Tablespoon chili powder

1 Tablespoon smoked paprika

1 tsp Liquid Smoke (optional for a deeper smoky flavor)

To Finish

1/4 Cup brown sugar

INSTRUCTIONS

1. Turn on the Sauté setting and add the ground beef, bacon, and onion. Cook until meat is no longer pink (you shouldn't have to drain it unless you use a fattier meat. Leave in a small amount of fat.)

2. Add the garlic and stir. Let cook for 1 minute. Add the water and kielbasa.

3. Then add remaining ingredients in order (except brown sugar), and do not stir, make sure it is covered with water.

4. Put the lid on the pot and set value to sealing and cancel the Sauté setting.

5. Select the Pressure Cook button at High Pressure for 8 minutes.

6. Watch the pot until it comes to pressure. This is a pretty thick mixture, so you want to make sure you don't get the burn message. If you do, remove the lid if the pin is still down (otherwise release any pressure first) and use a wood spoon to scrape the bottom. Add another 1/4 cup of water if it looks too thick, close the lid, and reset.

7. When the cook time is finished, turn the pot off and let it sit undisturbed for 15 minutes (Natural Release). Then release the remaining pressure in short bursts, until you are sure no sauce will be spewing out with the steam.

8. When the pressure is released, open and carefully mix up the beans. Stir in the brown sugar.

9. Serve with corn bread.

Fresh Green Beans & Potatoes

This is my go to side dish as well as a family favorite. This dish pairs with everything. On a vacation this year, I cooked this recipe for one of our dinners with friends. Everyone RAVED about how easy and delicious this dish was; not only to make – but to take! Word from our friends was that this dish taken to a church potluck and was a huge hit with ZERO leftovers!

PREP 10 MIN | COOK 6 MIN | QUICK RELEASE

INGREDIENTS

1 Tablespoon olive oil

4 Slices of bacon, chopped

1 Cup diced onions

5 cloves garlic, minced

3 Cups chicken broth

1/2 Teaspoon salt

1/2 Teaspoon coarsely ground black pepper

1/2 Teaspoon garlic powder

4 Tablespoons unsalted butter

1 Pound fresh green beans, trimmed and cut in half

24 ounce bag of small potatoes

INSTRUCTIONS

1. Turn pot on Sauté and add olive oil. Add chopped bacon and cook for about 3 minutes. Add onion and garlic and sauté until translucent.

2. Add ¼ cup of chicken broth and deglaze the bottom of the pot.

3. Add in salt, pepper, and garlic powder. Cut butter in cubes and put a 1/3 of the cubes in the pot. Add in half the potatoes and green beans, add another 1/3 of the butter. Then add in the other half of potatoes, green beans and the rest of butter on top. Pour remainder of chicken broth over the top. (You are creating a layered effect, so everything cooks and flavors evenly)

4. Secure and seal the lid. Turn valve to sealing position. Cook at High Pressure for 6 minutes. As soon as cooking is complete, quick release pressure. Uncover and stir.

5. Add additional salt and pepper to taste if needed. Serve while hot.

Garlic Parmesan Green Beans

Garlic Parmesan Green Beans are a fantastic side dish for any time of year. It will be especially welcome on your Easter dinner table with irresistible crisp-tender perfection and a generous helping of flavorful, crunchy garlic parmesan.

PREP 10 MIN | COOK 4 MIN | QUICK RELEASE

INGREDIENTS

1 Pound fresh green beans

1/4 Cup water

1 Teaspoon minced garlic dry

1/8 Teaspoon salt

1 Teaspoon unsalted butter

1/4 Cup grated parmesan cheese, in the shaker

INSTRUCTIONS

1. Snap off ends of the green beans and wash.
2. Add the water, garlic, salt and green beans to the Instant Pot. Place the butter on top of the green beans. Select Pressure Cook at High Pressure for 0 (Z-E-R-O) minutes.
3. Quick Release, when cooking completed.
4. Turn the Instant Pot onto Sauté and simmer until the liquid has evaporated. Once the liquid has evaporated, add in the parmesan cheese.
5. Scrape the bottom of the Instant Pot with your spoon as the cheese starts to melt. Keep scraping and scrape until you have golden brown parmesan cheese crumbles.

Green Bean Casserole

No holiday meal is complete without Green Bean Casserole. This recipe makes the same delicious recipe in much less time in the oven, making space for your other dishes.

PREP 10 MIN | COOK 20 MIN | QUICK RELEASE

INGREDIENTS

1 Tablespoon flour

2 Tablespoons water

2 Teaspoons olive oil

3 Cloves garlic, minced

1 Can, 10.5oz, cream of mushroom soup

5 Cups fresh green beans, stems removed

1/2 Cup mozzarella cheese, shredded

1 Cup sharp cheddar cheese, shredded

1 Cup mozzarella cheese, cut into small cubes

1/3 Cup panko breadcrumbs

1-1/2 Cup french-fried onions

1/2 Teaspoon salt

1/4 Teaspoon pepper

Cooking spray

INSTRUCTIONS

1. In small bowl, combine flour and water. Using small amounts of flour in the Instant Pot is fine. It is larger amounts that will cause sticking and burning to the pot.
2. Turn Instant Pot to Sauté setting. Add olive oil and garlic. Cook for 1–2 minutes.
3. Add cream of mushroom soup and green beans. Stir in salt and pepper.
4. Place lid on pot and seal. Select Pressure Cook at High Pressure for 12 minutes.
5. When cooking is complete, Quick Release steam.
6. Turn Instant Pot to Sauté. Add flour and water to pot.
7. Add 1/2 cup cheddar cheese and 1/4 cup shredded mozzarella. Stir and allow to sauté until cheese has melted.
8. Preheat oven to 425F. Spray large casserole dish with cooking spray.
9. Pour mixture into large casserole dish. Mix mozzarella cubes throughout casserole.
10. Top with remaining shredded cheese, panko breadcrumbs and fried onions.
11. Bake for 5–7 minutes, until browned.

Buttery Lima Beans with Bacon

Lima Beans, also called Butter Beans in the South, are an excellent source of iron. Helps keep us going with all our busy lives.

PREP 10 MIN | COOK 30 MIN | NATURAL RELEASE

INGREDIENTS

2/3 Cup cooked bacon pieces, cut into small pieces

1 Tablespoons butter

1/2 yellow onion

1/4 Cup light brown sugar

1 Pound dry lima beans

4 Cups chicken broth

1/4 Teaspoon salt

1/4 Teaspoon pepper

INSTRUCTIONS

1. Turn pot to sauté and cook bacon. Leave 1 Tablespoon of bacon fat and remove the rest.

2. Add butter and onion, cook about 5 minutes

3. Add in brown sugar and mix well.

4. Add a small amount of chicken broth and deglaze the bottom of the pan.

5. Put in the lima beans and rest of chicken broth.

6. Change setting to pressure cook, put on lid and make sure valve is on sealing.

7. Set Pressure Cook time for 30 minutes on high pressure.

8. When completed, Natural Release.

9. Stir beans well and add additional salt & pepper if needed.

Refried Beans

A simple combination of pinto beans, garlic, spices, and lime juice will give you restaurant quality refried beans in only 30 minutes.

PREP 10 MIN | COOK 30 MIN | NATURAL RELEASE

INGREDIENTS

2 Pounds dry pinto beans

1 large onion, chopped

4 Tablespoons minced garlic, from a jar

1 to 1 1/2 Tablespoons salt

1 Teaspoon black pepper

2 Teaspoon cumin

2 Teaspoon oregano

1 Teaspoon lime juice

1 Teaspoon chili powder

4 Cups chicken broth

1/2 Teaspoon apple cider vinegar (if not soaking beans)

INSTRUCTIONS

1. Sort and rinse the beans, removing any stones, dirt and shriveled beans. Note: To Soak: Cover beans with water, with about 2 inches of water over beans, and let sit 8 hours or overnight. NO Soak: add ½ teaspoon of apple cider vinegar after cooking, to aid with digestion.

2. Add beans and all the other ingredients.

3. Put on the Instant Pot lid, making sure that the valve is turned to sealing.

4. Select Pressure Cook at High Pressure for 30 minutes. When finished cooking, allow the Instant Pot to Naturally Release pressure.

5. Mash beans using a potato masher or immersion blender.

6. Beans will appear quite soupy, but will thicken up as they cool.

Red Beans & Rice with Sausage

New Orleans style red beans and rice is mind-bendingly delicious. Smoky, spicy, hearty, and supremely comforting.

PREP 15 MIN | COOK 55 MIN | NATURAL RELEASE

INGREDIENTS

1/4 Pound thick sliced bacon (2-3 slices)

1 1/2 Pounds Andouille sausage (or a good smoky Kielbasa) sliced in 3/4" rounds

1 Large yellow onion

2 Cups celery, diced

5 Cups chicken broth

7 Cloves garlic, minced

3 bay leaves

1 green bell pepper, chopped

1 red bell pepper, chopped

1/2 Teaspoon sage, dried

1/2 Teaspoon basil, dried

1 Tablespoon Cajun / creole seasoning

1 Pound small red beans sorted & rinsed (pinto beans work well too)

1/4 Cup parsley, chopped

2 Cups cooked white rice

Green Onions, for garnish (optional)

Hot Sauce, as much as you like

INSTRUCTIONS

1. Turn the pressure cooker on to the Sauté setting. Add the bacon and cook, stirring occasionally, until it renders the fat. Remove the bacon and set aside (You won't be adding it in, you just want the fat).

2. If you are using Andouille sausage, add it and brown on both sides. Then remove. If using kielbasa, don't brown it, add it with the beans.

3. Add the onions, celery and a splash of broth. Cook for a couple of minutes, to deglaze the bottom of the pot.

4. Add the garlic, bay leaves, green and red bell peppers, sage, and basil. Stir frequently, until onion is translucent. Add the Cajun/Creole seasoning, and stir.

5. Add the broth, beans, and sausage. Stir and put the lid on the pot and lock. Set the valve to the Sealing position. Cancel the Sauté function, select Pressure Cook, and add 40 minutes at High Pressure.

6. When the cooking cycle has finished, let the pot sit undisturbed for 20 minutes. Then quick release the remaining pressure. Remove lid. Carefully stir the beans with a long handled spoon.

7. Taste a few of the beans to make sure they are tender. If not, close the lid and cook for 5 more minutes.

8. Mash some of the beans and stir to make a more creamy consistency. Taste and add more seasoning if desired. Stir in the chopped parsley.

9. Serve over cooked white rice and garnish with green onions and hot sauce.

Sugar Snap Peas

Here is an incredibly simple, incredibly fast side dish that makes the most of great ingredients.

PREP 5 MIN | COOK 10 MIN | QUICK RELEASE

INGREDIENTS

11/2 Teaspoon olive oil

1 Cup chicken broth

2 Cups whole sugar snap peas

salt as needed

black pepper as needed

For topping

1 Tablespoon peanuts

1 Teaspoon sesame seeds

1 Tablespoon pumpkin seeds

1/4 Teaspoon garlic powder

1 Teaspoon raisins

Lemon juice as needed

INSTRUCTIONS

1. Add the olive oil, 1 cup chicken broth, sugar snap peas, salt, and black pepper as needed to your instant pot.

2. Select Pressure Cook on High Pressure for 0 (ZERO) minutes and release pressure immediately.

3. While they are cooking, roast the ingredients for topping on stove until you get a nice aroma. (peanuts, sesame, pumpkin seeds) In the food processor, coarsely chop the peanuts.

4. Sprinkle the crushed peanuts, sesame seeds, pumpkin seeds, garlic powder, raisins, lemon juice on the sugar snap peas and serve.

Tomatillo Poblano White Beans

These tomatillo poblano white beans are a warm stew of perfectly creamy beans, tart tomatillos, spicy poblano pepper, onion, cumin, and oregano.

PREP 5 MIN | COOK 35 MIN | NATURAL RELEASE

INGREDIENTS

2 Cups tomatillos, chopped

1 Cup poblano, seed and stems removed before chopping

1 Cup onion, chopped

1/2 Jalapeño, without seeds, or use more to turn up the heat

1 1/2 Teaspoon ground cumin

1 1/2 Cups Great Northern beans, dried

1 1/2 Cups water

2 Teaspoon dried oregano

Salt and Pepper to taste

INSTRUCTIONS

1. Turn on sauté function on instant pot to warm up, add the tomatillos, poblano, onion and jalapeño to your blender or food processor. Pulse until the veggies are in tiny pieces, but not pureed.

2. Pour in the blended veggies; add the cumin and stir to combine. Sauté for about 4 minutes.

3. Add the beans, water and oregano to the sauté mixture and stir to combine. Put the lid on and turn Valve to sealing. Pressure Cook at high pressure for 35 minutes.

4. Allow the pressure to release naturally.

5. If there is still more liquid in the pot than you'd like to have, switch back to the sauté setting and simmer to allow some of the liquid to evaporate.

6. Add salt and pepper to taste before serving.

Pasta Recipes

In order to create a little bit of confidence, start cooking with pasta.
Pasta is phenomenal. Once you've cooked pasta properly for the first time
it becomes second nature.

-Gordon Ramsay

Beef Enchilada Pasta

The flavors of enchiladas with the family friendly comfort of pasta.
This recipe is sure to make it into your regular rotation.

PREP 5 MIN | COOK 4 MIN | NATURAL RELEASE

INGREDIENTS

1 lb. ground beef

1-1/2 cups rotini, uncooked

1 Tablespoon chili powder

1 1/2 teaspoons cumin

10-oz can enchilada sauce

2 cups beef broth

1/4-1/2 cup of water (if needed)

1 can black beans, drained

1-1/2 cups shredded cheddar cheese

INSTRUCTIONS

1. In the Instant Pot, brown ground beef using the Sauté setting.

2. Once beef is cooked, drain excess grease if necessary and return beef to insert pot.

3. Add pasta in a layer on top of the beef. DO NOT STIR. Sprinkle chili powder and cumin over the pasta.

4. Pour enchilada sauce and beef broth over the pasta. DO NOT STIR. Use a spoon to press down any pieces of pasta so that they are fully covered with liquid. If necessary, add 1/4-1/2 cup of water to ensure that the pasta is just barely covered with liquid.

5. Add beans on top. DO NOT STIR.

6. Close lid and set vent to the sealed position. Cook for 4 minutes at high pressure, using Pressure Cook function.

7. Once cook time is complete, allow a Natural Release for 5 minutes, followed by a quick release of remaining pressure. Once pressure has released, carefully remove lid and stir.

8. Add in shredded cheese, stirring until melted. Contents will be somewhat soupy initially, but the liquid will thicken and become more sauce-like as the cheese melts and the mixture cools a bit more.

9. Serve, topping with additional shredded cheese if desired.

Beef Stroganoff

Beef stroganoff is the ultimate cold weather dinner. Usually, dishes this hearty take hours of simmering or braising, but not ours. With a few flavor-building tips, you're less than an hour away from perfect stroganoff, which makes it perfect for weeknights.

PREP 10 MIN | COOK 30 MIN | QUICK RELEASE

INGREDIENTS

1/3 cup flour

2 teaspoons salt

¼ teaspoon black pepper

1/4 teaspoon garlic powder

1/4 teaspoon nutmeg

2 pounds chuck roast or stew meat cubed

2 Tablespoons vegetable oil

1 large onion sliced

8 ounces mushrooms sliced

1/4 cup red wine

1/4 cup cooking sherry

3 cups low-sodium beef broth

1 (12-ounce) package wide egg noodles

3/4 cup sour cream

3 tablespoons chopped fresh parsley leaves

Salt and pepper to taste

INSTRUCTIONS

1. In a large bowl, combine flour, salt, pepper, garlic powder and nutmeg. Pat beef dry with paper towels and add to the flour mixture in the bowl; toss to coat.

2. Set Instant Pot to Sauté, add vegetable oil and brown the meat on all sides. Meat will not be cooked through. Transfer browned meat onto a plate.

3. Add onion and mushrooms, cook, stirring occasionally, until tender, about 5-6 minutes.

4. Stir in sherry and red wine, deglaze the bottom of the pot.

5. Stir in beef broth and return beef to Instant Pot.

6. Cover and seal the lid, Select Pressure Cook at High Pressure for 12 minutes. When finished, Quick Release the pressure before removing the lid.

7. Add the egg noodles. Cover and seal the lid, turn the vent to sealing. Press the Pressure Cook at High Pressure for 5 minutes. When finished, quick-release the pressure.

8. Stir in sour cream and parsley and season with salt and pepper, to taste.

Broccoli & Cheddar Pasta

*Broccoli & Cheese Pasta is a classic American dish that can be a stand-alone meal;
Or used as a hearty side dish.*

PREP 1 MIN | COOK 5 MIN | QUICK RELEASE

INGREDIENTS

1 pound of pasta
4 cups chicken broth
1 cup frozen broccoli
1 cup milk
16 oz. cheddar cheese

INSTRUCTIONS

1. Place chicken broth and pasta in your Instant pot.
2. Place frozen broccoli in a steamer on top of pasta.
3. Select Pressure Cook on High Pressure for 5 minutes.
4. When cooking is complete, do a Quick Release.
5. Turn pot to Sauté function and add in milk and cheese. Stir until cheese is melted.
6. Serve immediately.

Buffalo Chicken Pasta

Instant Pot Buffalo Chicken Pasta is zesty, rich, and delicious! The flavor is like that of Buffalo Chicken Wings, only in a bowl of creamy, cheesy pasta! This pressure cooker Buffalo Chicken Pasta is easy to make, and is great for a weeknight meal, or for a Game Day party!

PREP 10 MIN | COOK 6 MIN | QUICK RELEASE

INGREDIENTS

- 3 1/2 cups Chicken Broth
- 1 (12 oz.) box Farfalle Pasta
- 8 oz. Cream Cheese, cubed
- 1/2 cup Celery, diced (optional)
- 2 Chicken Breasts, boneless/skinless cut in half crossways (or 3 cups cooked shredded chicken)
- 1/3 cup Buffalo Hot Wing Sauce (such as Frank's Red Hot) plus extra for garnish
- 1/2 cup Ranch Dressing
- 1 cup Cheddar Cheese, shredded
- Green Onion, for garnish
- Crumbled Bleu Cheese, for garnish

INSTRUCTIONS

1. Pour the chicken broth into the pot.
2. Pour in the pasta and even out the layer.
3. Place the cubes of cream cheese and celery evenly over the pasta, do not stir.
4. Place the chicken breast pieces on top of the cream cheese/pasta (If using cooked chicken, add it after pressure cooking).
5. Pour the buffalo hot wing sauce over the chicken & pasta/cream cheese. Do not stir.
6. Place the lid on the pot and lock into place, setting the steam release valve to the Sealing position.
7. Select Pressure Cook on High Pressure for 6 minutes.
8. When the cook time has ended, do a Quick Release of the pressure. When pressure released, open the lid and remove the chicken to a plate. Stir the pasta mixture well until the cream cheese lumps have mixed in.
9. Shred the chicken with two forks and add back into the pot. (Add cooked chicken in here)
10. Add the cheese and stir.
11. Add Ranch dressing and stir until well combined.
12. Garnish with green onion and crumbled Bleu Cheese. Add extra hot wing sauce or dressing, if desired.

Butternut Squash Ravioli

This creamy butternut squash ravioli is one of the best Instant Pot pasta recipes to try in the fall.

PREP 5 MIN | COOK 25 MIN | QUICK RELEASE

INGREDIENTS

2 tablespoons olive oil

3 ½ cups cubed butternut squash

1 shallot, chopped

5 cups chicken broth

20 oz. ravioli* (See Note)

3 fresh sage leaves (or ½ teaspoon dried sage)

1 teaspoon salt

¼ cup heavy cream

½ cup freshly grated parmesan cheese

INSTRUCTIONS

1. Set the Instant Pot to sauté and heat olive oil in the pot.
2. Add shallot and butternut squash. Sauté for 3 minutes, stirring occasionally.
3. Add broth, ravioli*, sage and salt.
4. Set to Pressure Cook at High Pressure for 10 minutes.
5. When cooking is completed, Quick Release, so you don't overcook ravioli.
6. Remove the sage leaves.
7. Carefully stir everything. It'll be soupy, but don't worry. Butternut squash will fall apart and thicken everything, as you stir.
8. Stir in cream and Parmesan cheese. Salt and pepper to taste.
9. Mix everything and let it sit for 10-15 minutes, covered. The sauce will thicken and be absorbed into ravioli, as it rests.
10. *NOTE: You can use fresh or frozen ravioli, with the filling of your choice. I normally use a cheese-filled with this recipe.

Cheesy Rosemary Orzo

Tender orzo pasta is infused with the flavor of Rosemary and finished off with savory Parmesan cheese in this tasty side dish that perfectly complements your main entrée.

PREP 10 MIN | COOK 4 MIN | QUICK RELEASE

INGREDIENTS

2 teaspoons Olive Oil

2 teaspoons Butter

1/2 small Onion, diced

3 cloves Garlic

1/2 teaspoons Salt (or more to taste)

2 cups Chicken Broth

8 oz. Orzo Pasta

1 1/2 cups Grated Parmesan Cheese

1 cup Mozzarella Cheese, shredded

1 cup Half & Half

2 Sprigs of Fresh Rosemary

INSTRUCTIONS

1. Turn on your pressure cooker's Sauté function, add the olive oil and butter.
2. Add the onions and cook until translucent, stirring occasionally.
3. Add the garlic and cook for about 30 seconds, stirring constantly.
4. Add the salt and broth. Stir, and let come to a simmer.
5. Stir in the Orzo and Rosemary. Then place the lid on, locking in place. Set the Steam Release Valve to sealing position.
6. Press the Pressure Cook/Manual button set for 4 minutes.
7. When cooking is complete, immediately Quick Release. When all of the steam has vented, and the pin in the lid drops down, open the lid.
8. Stir in the parmesan cheese, then stir in the mozzarella.
9. Stir in the half and half.
10. Serve immediately, garnish with any leftover fresh rosemary.

Natalie's Chicken Alfredo Pasta

This is my daughter's favorite meal to order when we go out. I wanted to create a meal at home that was just as good for her, and now she'd rather I make her this than go out! WIN!

PREP 15 MIN | COOK 6 MIN | QUICK RELEASE

INGREDIENTS

kosher salt and freshly ground black pepper

1/2 Teaspoon garlic powder

2 large chicken breasts (about 1.5 Pounds)

2 Tablespoons olive oil

4 cloves of garlic minced

1 quart chicken broth

1 pint heavy cream

1 Pound of uncooked penne pasta

8oz of freshly shredded real parmesan cheese

fresh parsley minced for garnish

INSTRUCTIONS

1. Season chicken breasts with salt, pepper and garlic powder.
2. Set Instant Pot to Sauté function, add olive oil to pot and sear chicken for several minutes on both sides until evenly browned.
3. Remove chicken from pot and set aside to be added back in with the rest of the ingredients.
4. Add garlic to pot and cook for about one minute.
5. Add chicken broth and use wooden spoon to scrape up browned bits from the bottom of the pot.
6. Add heavy cream, uncooked pasta, a teaspoon of kosher salt and several turns of freshly ground pepper.
7. Return chicken breasts to Instant Pot and stir all ingredients together.
8. Cancel Sauté function, then lock lid in place with valve set to sealing.
9. Select Pressure Cook on High Pressure for 6 minutes. Once cooking is complete, use Quick Release to release steam.
10. Remove chicken breast, stir pasta and cream mixture together and slowly add in freshly grated parmesan cheese.
11. Slice chicken breast, return to pot and combine with pasta.
12. Serve with additional freshly ground pepper, shredded parmesan and chopped parsley.

Creamy Chicken Rigatoni

My family could live on pasta alone, especially when it's covered in a creamy marinara sauce.

PREP 5 MIN | COOK 5 MIN | QUICK RELEASE

INGREDIENTS

1 Tablespoon olive oil

1 Pound chicken cut into bite size pieces

Salt and pepper to taste

1/4 Teaspoon garlic powder

1/2 Pound rigatoni pasta

2 bell peppers cut into large pieces

1 yellow onion sliced

24 oz. marinara sauce keep jar to fill half way with water

3/4 Cup half & half

1/2 Cup parmesan cheese

2-3 Tablespoons fresh basil

1/2 Teaspoon red pepper flakes optional

INSTRUCTIONS

1. Press Sauté function and heat Instant Pot. Add olive oil. Once pot says HOT, add chicken. Sprinkle with salt, pepper, garlic powder and then let cook till brown on one side, about 2-3 minutes. Stir and make sure no chicken pieces are sticking to the bottom. Hit cancel.

2. Add peppers and onions on top of the chicken. Add pasta. Add marinara sauce and then fill jar halfway and add water, about 1 cup. Push any noodles that are above the sauce into it.

3. Put lid on the Instant Pot and turn valve to sealing. Select Pressure Cook at High Pressure for 5 minutes. Once finished, do a quick release.

4. Add the half & half and parmesan cheese. Stir to distribute.

5. Add basil, red pepper flakes and serve.

Creamy Italian Sausage Tortellini

A quick recipe that can be made with just a few ingredients. It is correct that the cook time is "0", because it cooks in the time it take the Instant Pot to come to pressure. These fantastic tortellini's come out like you've been in the kitchen cooking all day.

PREP 15 MIN | COOK 0 MIN | NATURAL RELEASE

INGREDIENTS

1 Pound ground Italian sausage

1 yellow onion, diced

1 Cup beef broth

19oz package frozen cheese tortellini

28oz can crushed tomatoes

1/2 Cup Half & Half

1/2 Cup grated mozzarella cheese for garnish

INSTRUCTIONS

1. Turn your Instant Pot to the sauté setting. When the display says HOT add in the sausage. Break it up with a wooden spoon, then add in the diced onion.

2. Once the sausage is browned and the onions are soft, add in the beef broth and deglaze the pot.

3. Pour the frozen tortellini evenly over the top. Add the tomatoes evenly over the top of the tortellini and don't stir.

4. Cover the pot and secure the lid. Turn the valve to sealing. Select the Pressure Cook at High Pressure for zero minutes.

5. When the time is up let the pot Natural Release for 5 minutes and then quick release the rest of pressure. Remove the lid.

6. Stir in the half & half.

7. Serve into bowls and add 1/2 Tablespoon of mozzarella cheese, if desired.

Creamy Ziti

All the heartiness of baked ziti just got easier, thanks to the Instant Pot. Despite coming together in no time, this dish is creamy, and, most importantly, tastes like it's been simmering all day long.

PREP 14 MIN | COOK 6 MIN | NATURAL RELEASE

INGREDIENTS

1 1/2 cup chicken broth

1 cup heavy cream

1 tsp minced garlic, dried

salt and pepper to taste

8 oz. dry ziti pasta

1 cup red pasta sauce (any brand)

1 cup parmesan cheese, shredded

1/2 cup mozzarella cheese, shredded

INSTRUCTIONS

1. Add the broth, cream, garlic, salt, pepper and noodles to the instant pot in that order. DO NOT STIR, but make sure all noodles are covered.

2. Set your Instant Pot to Pressure Cook at High Pressure for 6 minutes. When cooking is completed, let it naturally release pressure.

3. Add the red pasta sauce to the Instant Pot and give it a stir.

4. SLOWLY add in the cheese while stirring. The cheese will melt and thicken the sauce. The sauce will also thicken as it cools.

5. Serve immediately.

Hamburger Mac

Running in quick from work and have to go right back out to after school practices with kids? This is a perfect dinner to give everyone a good protein boost and fill them up with energy.

PREP 5 MIN | COOK 10 MIN | NATURAL RELEASE

INGREDIENTS

1 Pound extra lean ground beef

1/2 Teaspoon garlic powder

1/2 Teaspoon smoked paprika

1/2 Teaspoon onion powder

1/4 Teaspoon ground cumin

1 Tablespoon Worcestershire sauce

1 Pound uncooked macaroni elbows

4 Cups chicken broth

4 Cups grated sharp cheddar

2 Cups grated Gouda (or Havarti, Provolone or other melty white cheese)

Salt & pepper to taste

INSTRUCTIONS

1. Choose the Sauté function, and add the beef garlic powder, smoked paprika, onion powder, ground cumin, and Worcestershire sauce in your Instant Pot.

2. Sauté for 5-7 minutes. Stir and break the beef up with your wooden spoon as you go along. Most of the liquid should be evaporated before you move onto the next step.

3. Add the macaroni and water to the Instant Pot. Give it a good stir. Close the lid and make sure the valve is set to sealing. Select Pressure Cook at High Pressure for 5 minute.

4. While pot is cooking, grate your cheeses.

5. Once cooking is complete, let steam pressure release naturally.

6. Stir in the cheeses (a large wooden spoon works well for this). I like to stir in about a third of the cheese at a time until it's nice and creamy, and then repeat until all the cheese has been used.

7. Season with salt & pepper as needed. Serve immediately.

Chicken Jalapeño Popper Pasta

Creamy chicken pasta loaded with bacon, jalapeños, and pepper jack cheese. Everyone cleaned their plate! Even our picky eaters!!

PREP 10 MIN | COOK 4 MIN | QUICK RELEASE

INGREDIENTS

2 Tablespoons olive oil

1-Pound boneless, skinless chicken breast, cut into bite-sized pieces

2 to 3 jalapeños, chopped

2 Teaspoons dried minced onion

1/4 Teaspoon garlic powder

salt and pepper, to taste

1-Pound dry penne pasta

3 Cups chicken broth

2 Cups water

1/2 Cup cooked chopped bacon

1 (8-oz) package cream cheese

2 Cups (8-oz) shredded pepper jack cheese

INSTRUCTIONS

1. Warm Instant Pot on Sauté setting; add oil, chicken, jalapeños, minced onions, and garlic powder, stirring to coat. Cook chicken 2–3 minutes.

2. Add pasta, broth, and water to the pot.

3. Close lid, lock pot, select Pressure Cook at High Pressure for 4 minutes. When cooking is complete, then Quick Release pressure.

4. Open lid, stir in cream cheese, pepper jack cheese, and cooked bacon until combined; let the pasta sit 5 minutes to thicken.

5. Serve immediately.

Lemon Parmesan Orzo

A splash of lemon and shower of chopped parsley brighten this orzo, one of my family's most requested springtime sides. It's fantastic with chicken, pork and fish, or you can eat it on its own as a light lunch.

PREP 5 MIN | COOK 20 MIN | QUICK RELEASE

INGREDIENTS

2 Tablespoons butter

1 1/2 Cup Orzo pasta

3 cloves garlic minced

2 3/4 Cups chicken broth

1 Cup parmesan grated

3 Tablespoons parsley chopped

1 Cup cherry tomatoes washed and sliced in half

2 Tablespoons lemon juice

Salt to taste

Black Pepper to taste

INSTRUCTIONS

1. Warm Instant Pot in Sauté mode. Add butter and orzo pasta. Sauté for about 3 minutes until some orzo pieces turn golden brown. Stir continuously, or it can burn.

2. Add garlic and stir it in with the toasted orzo.

3. Add broth and stir well. Press cancel and close lid with vent in sealing position.

4. Pressure cook at high pressure for 3 minutes. When the cooking time is done, quick release the pressure.

5. Open the instant pot, then add parmesan, parsley, cherry tomatoes and lemon juice. Stir well and let it sit for 2-3 minutes.

6. Add salt and pepper to taste.

MACARONI & CHEESE

This Mac and Cheese is a family favorite recipe, loved by both children and adults. Perfect for a comforting dinner or as a holiday side dish!

PREP 5 MIN | COOK 5 MIN | QUICK RELEASE

INGREDIENTS

2 1/2 Cups uncooked elbow macaroni noodles

1 Cup vegetable broth

2 Cups water

3 Tablespoons butter, cut into cubes

1/4 Teaspoon salt

1/4 Teaspoon pepper

1/4 Teaspoon garlic powder

2 Cups freshly grated sharp cheddar cheese

1/3 Cup milk (whole or 2%)

1/3 Cup heavy cream

INSTRUCTIONS

1. Add the macaroni, vegetable broth, water, butter, garlic powder, pepper, and salt to the Instant Pot.

2. Place the lid on the pot and set valve to sealing. Cook on Pressure Cook on High Pressure for 4 minutes.

3. When cooking is complete, Do a Quick Release of pressure.

4. Stir in heavy cream, milk, and cheese, and stir until creamy and thick.

5. Serve and Enjoy!

Pesto Chicken Pasta

You can't go wrong with a bowl of pesto chicken pasta for dinner! This chicken pesto pasta is ready in under 30 minutes and is packed fresh flavors.

PREP 15 MIN | COOK 15 MIN | QUICK RELEASE

INGREDIENTS

1 Tablespoon olive oil

2 medium-sized chicken breasts, diced

3 cloves garlic, minced

4 Cups chicken broth

1 Pound rotini pasta, uncooked

1/2 Teaspoon salt

1 Cup parmesan cheese, grated

1 jar of store-bought pesto

1 red pepper, diced

1 small red onion, diced

1 head broccoli, chopped

INSTRUCTIONS

1. In the following order add olive oil, chicken, garlic, water and pasta to Instant Pot, making sure most of pasta is submerged just below the surface of the water.

2. Select Pressure Cook on High Pressure for 3 minutes. Once cooking is complete, do a Quick Release of the pressure and remove lid.

3. Stir in salt, parmesan cheese, pesto, red pepper, red onion and broccoli, mixing well. Place lid back on and let sit 10 minutes to steam the veggies.

4. Serve immediately.

Sailor's Garlic Parmesan Pasta

This is my husband's famous pasta. Well... famous according to all the kids in our neighborhood. They all want to eat with us when Sailor's Pasta is on the menu.

PREP 5 MIN | COOK 4 MIN | NATURAL RELEASE

INGREDIENTS

1-pound box of favorite pasta, uncooked (rotini is our "go to")

2 Cups of Chicken Broth

4 Tablespoons butter, cut into 16 pieces

1 Tablespoon Italian seasoning

1/2 cup Parmesan cheese, (shaker)

INSTRUCTIONS

1. Add in pasta and chicken broth. (make sure pasta is completely covered with broth, add more if needed)

2. Close lid, make sure vent is closed to sealing and use the Pressure Cook function. Add 4 minutes at high pressure. Once complete, Natural release pressure.

3. Thoroughly drain pasta and return to Instant pot. Add butter pieces and stir until melted and all pasta is coated.

4. Add Italian seasoning and Parmesan cheese, stir thoroughly.

5. Serve with your favorite entrée.

Shrimp & Vodka Sauce Pasta

This Shrimp Penne with Vodka Sauce is an easy dinner for two.

PREP 3 MIN | COOK 6 MIN | QUICK RELEASE

INGREDIENTS

1 Tablespoon butter

1/2 Cup chopped onion

4 cloves garlic, minced

1/4-1/2 Teaspoon crushed red pepper

28oz crushed tomatoes

3 Cups water

1/2 Cup vodka

16 ounces dried penne pasta, uncooked

¾ teaspoon salt

16 ounces large raw shrimp, peeled and deveined

1/2 Cup heavy cream

Salt and pepper to taste

Garnish: Parmesan cheese

INSTRUCTIONS

1. Set the pressure cooker on Sauté. Add the butter, onions, garlic, and crushed red pepper. Sauté for 3-5 minutes to soften the onions, stirring occasionally.

2. Add in the crushed tomatoes, water, vodka, penne, and 3/4 teaspoons salt. Stir to coat the pasta.

3. Cover and lock the lid into place. Set the Instant Pot on Pressure Cook at High Pressure for 4 minutes. Once it is finished cooking, Quick Release the steam.

4. Unlock the lid and stir the shrimp and cream into the pasta. Set the Instant Pot on Sauté and cook for 2-3 minutes, until the shrimp are pink. Taste, then salt and pepper as needed.

5. Serve warm with Parmesan cheese, if desired.

Spaghetti & Meat Sauce

An easy meat sauce recipe for spaghetti made quickly with ground beef and pasta sauce, flavored with onion and garlic.

PREP 10 MIN | COOK 20 MIN | NATURAL RELEASE

INGREDIENTS

2 Tablespoons olive oil

½ Cup chopped onion

2 cloves garlic, finely chopped

1 Pound ground beef

½ Teaspoon Italian seasoning

Pinch of crushed red pepper, or to taste

Kosher salt and fresh cracked black pepper

3 Cups water

1 Teaspoon kosher salt

1 Pound spaghetti, broken in half

3 Cups marinara sauce

Freshly grated Parmigiano-Reggiano, for serving

INSTRUCTIONS

1. Turn on Sauté and heat olive oil until hot. Add onions and cook until translucent. Add garlic and stir for just a bit until fragrant.

2. Add ground beef and continue cooking and stirring to break up clumps until browned and no longer pink.

3. Add the Italian seasoning, crushed red pepper and a sprinkle of salt and pepper. Stir to combine and cook another minute.

4. Turn off sauté setting. Add water and salt to the pot. Lay spaghetti on top and then cover with marinara sauce. With tongs, carefully and gently toss to combine, making sure all the spaghetti is covered with liquid.

5. Secure lid and seal Instant Pot. Select Pressure Cook on High Pressure for 6 minutes. When finished, let pressure naturally release for 6 more minutes. Quick release remaining pressure and carefully remove lid.

6. With tongs, stir and toss to combine spaghetti and sauce, carefully breaking up any clumps of pasta.

7. Taste and add addition salt, if needed.

8. Serve with plenty of freshly grated Parmesan.

Spinach & Mushroom Lasagna

Vegetarian Lasagna to feed a crowd! This one is filled with mushrooms, spinach, and ricotta and Mozzarella cheeses. Your vegetarian and meat-eating guests will fight for seconds.

PREP 15 MIN | COOK 40 MIN | NATURAL RELEASE

INGREDIENTS

1 tablespoon oil

1 medium red onion, chopped

4-5 cloves garlic

1 Cup white mushrooms, diced

3 heaping cups fresh spinach

1 Cup ricotta

1/2 Cup parmesan

1/2 Teaspoon dried oregano

1/2 Teaspoon dried rosemary

1/2 Teaspoon salt, or to taste

1/4 Teaspoon black pepper, or to taste

1/2 Teaspoon red chili flakes, optional, for heat

7 no-boil lasagna noodles

1 Cup marinara sauce, divided

1 1/2 Cups shredded mozzarella cheese, divided

INSTRUCTIONS

1. Select Sauté mode on your Instant Pot. Once the oil is hot, add the onion and garlic.

2. Cook for 2 minutes until softened, then add the mushrooms. Cook for 4-5 minutes until mushrooms turn brown and release all their moisture.

3. Add the chopped spinach and mix. Cook for around 3 more minutes until all moisture dries out.

4. Transfer the mixture to a large bowl. Add ricotta cheese, parmesan, dried oregano, dried rosemary, salt, pepper and red chili flakes.

5. Mix until well combined. The veggie mixture is now ready.

6. Lightly grease a 7-inch Springform pan with oil. Divide the mushroom spinach mixture equally into 3 parts.

7. Start by layering the bottom of the pan with few of the noodles. You will need to break the noodles to fit them into the pan. Then apply a layer of marinara sauce.

8. Top with one portion of the spinach mushroom mixture and then 1/2 cup mozzarella cheese.

9. Repeat with another layer of noodles, sauce, spinach mushroom mixture, cheese.

10. Then repeat one more layer of noodles, sauce, spinach mushroom mixture and end with a thick layer of sauce.

11. Finally top the lasagna with 1/2 cup of mozzarella

cheese. You can use 3/4 cup of mozzarella on top if you like it extra cheesy. Cover pan with a foil so that no condensation falls into the lasagna when it pressure cooks.

12. Place 1 cup water in inner steel pot of the Instant Pot. Place a trivet inside the instant pot and then lift the pan using a sling (made by folding a long piece of aluminum foil length wise) and place it inside the pot. Close the lid.

13. Select Pressure Cook on high pressure for 22 minutes with the pressure valve in the sealing position. When cooking is complete, let the pressure release naturally.

14. Lift the lasagna carefully from the pot using the sling. Remove the foil from top, be careful of not letting any water fall into the lasagna pan.

15. Let it sit for 10 minutes before serving. At this point, I like to broil my lasagna for 2-3 minutes for the cheese to brown. It's optional and you may skip it.

Taco Pasta

*Taco Pasta is creamy, spicy and an easy Italian meets Mexican dinner.
I love making this pasta when I want everyone to come running to the table.*

PREP 5 MIN | COOK 20 MIN | QUICK RELEASE

INGREDIENTS

1 Pound lean ground beef

2 1/2 Tablespoons taco seasoning

16oz Salsa

16oz pasta shells, medium size

4 Cups beef broth

1 Cup shredded Monterey Jack

1 Cup shredded sharp cheddar

INSTRUCTIONS

1. Turn pot on to Sauté mode. When display reads Hot, add ground beef. Cook until mostly done.
2. Add the taco seasoning, stir and finish cooking meat.
3. Add the salsa and broth. Stir. Let the broth heat up and start to simmer.
4. Add the pasta and stir.
5. Cancel the sauté mode. Put the pressure cooker lid on and set the steam release valve to the sealing position.
6. Select the Pressure Cook at High Pressure for 4 minutes.
7. When cooking is complete, Quick Release the steam.
8. Give the pasta a good stir, add the cheese, stir again, and serve.
9. Garnish with any of these, if desired: Avocado, Jalapeño, Sour Cream, Tortilla Chips, Cilantro.

Traditional Lasagna

A traditional lasagna, with about half the time and effort!

PREP 10 MIN | COOK 20 MIN | NATURAL RELEASE

INGREDIENTS

Cheese Layer:

1 Cup Ricotta cheese

2 large eggs

1 Cup shredded Mozzarella cheese

1 Teaspoon dried basil

1 Teaspoon dried oregano

1 Teaspoon dried thyme

1 Teaspoon Italian Seasoning

1/4 Teaspoon salt

1/4 Teaspoon ground black pepper

Meat Layer:

1 Pound of ground beef

1 small onion diced

1 Tablespoon minced garlic

1 - 24 oz jar of pasta sauce

9 No-boil lasagna noodles

1 Cup shredded mozzarella cheese

For cooking in the Instant Pot:

1 1/2 Cups of water

INSTRUCTIONS

1. Mix all ingredients listed in the "Cheese Layer" section of the ingredients list. Stir to combine and set aside.
2. Turn on sauté function on Instant Pot and brown beef until no longer pink.
3. Add onion and minced garlic into pot and cook until onions are translucent.
4. Layer ingredients in the following order into a 7 inch Springform cake pan:
5. Layer One: Cover the bottom of the assembled Springform pan with about 3-4 broken no-boil noodles.
6. Layer Two: Thoroughly cover the noodles with 1 cup of the pasta sauce.
7. Layer Three: Spread 1/2 of the meat mixture evenly on top of the sauce layer. Press slightly.
8. Layer Four: Spread 1/2 of the cheese mixture evenly on top of the meat layer. Press slightly.
9. Repeat all 4 steps.
10. Add a final layer of no-boil lasagna noodles. Press slightly. Cover with sauce and sprinkle 1/2 cup of mozzarella cheese on top.
11. Spray a sheet of foil with nonstick spray and cover the pan.
12. Add 1 1/2 cup of water to the pot.

13. Place the covered lasagna pan on a trivet with handles then place it in the pot.

14. Lock the lid and seal valve. Press the Pressure Cook and set time to 25 minutes.

15. After cooking, allow natural release for 10 minutes. Then, perform a quick release. Open the Instant Pot and transfer the lasagna out.

16. Remove foil. Place on baking sheet in oven on broil until cheese begins to brown. Watch it closely so it doesn't burn, about 5 minutes.

17. Remove the lasagna from the oven, and let it rest on a cooling rack for 15 minutes. This will help maintain its shape when you try to remove it from the pan.

18. Release the lasagna from the sides of the Springform pan.

19. Garnish with fresh parsley if desired. Slice and serve.

Vegetable Lo Mein

Vegetable Lo Mein are soft and silky noodles covered in delicious Chinese Lo Mein sauce.

PREP 10 MIN | COOK 5 MIN | QUICK RELEASE

INGREDIENTS

1 garlic clove minced

1 Tablespoon sesame oil

8 oz. linguine pasta broken in half

1 Cup snow peas trimmed

1 Cup broccoli florets

2 carrots peeled and sliced into matchsticks

1 1/2 Cups chicken broth

1 Teaspoon grated ginger

2 Tablespoons low sodium soy sauce

1 Tablespoon oyster sauce

1 Tablespoon rice wine

1 Tablespoon light brown sugar

INSTRUCTIONS

1. Add garlic and sesame oil to the inner pot within your Instant Pot. Set to Sauté function and when the pot is heated, cook garlic until lightly browned. Cancel Sauté. Spread noodles across the bottom of the pot. Add vegetables on top.

2. In a medium bowl, add chicken broth, ginger, soy sauce, oyster sauce, rice wine and brown sugar. Whisk until evenly combined. Taste and adjust as needed. Pour sauce into the pot.

3. Seal your Instant Pot and set to Pressure Cook at High Pressure for 5 minutes.

4. When Instant Pot is done cooking, do a Quick Release. Remove the lid from Instant Pot. Initially, your noodles will look watery. Stir the noodles several times, breaking up any that may have clumped together during cooking. During this stirring, you should see that the water is quickly evaporating. Stir until all the water is gone.

5. Serve Immediately.

Rice Recipes

One cannot think well, love well, and sleep well if one has not dined well.

-*Virginia Woolf*

Basmati & Jasmine White Rice

This is the recipe I use for perfect rice every time. I always use chicken broth because we like the flavor it gives. You can substitute any flavor of broth, stock or even water.

PREP 20 MIN | COOK 4 MIN | QUICK RELEASE

INGREDIENTS

2 Cups rice

2 Cups chicken broth

INSTRUCTIONS

1. Soak rice for 20 minutes, then rinse.
2. Add rice and chicken broth to the Instant Pot.
3. Close the lid, seal valve, select Pressure Cook at High Pressure and for 4 minutes.
4. When cooking is complete, Quick Release pressure. Carefully, open lid and fluff rice with a fork.

Brown Rice

Preparing this rice is the same as the white, it just has a higher cooking time. If you are looking for a healthy alternative to white rice, this is a great recipe.

PREP 5 MIN | COOK 22 MIN | NATURAL RELEASE

INGREDIENTS

2 Cups brown rice

2 1/2 Cups chicken broth

INSTRUCTIONS

1. Soak rice for 20 minutes, then rinse.
2. Add rice and chicken broth to the Instant Pot.
3. Close the lid, seal valve, select Pressure Cook at High Pressure and for 4 minutes.
4. When cooking is complete, Quick Release pressure. Carefully, open lid and fluff rice with a fork.

Cajun Rice

This is the recipe I use for perfect rice every time. I always use chicken broth because we like the flavor it gives. You can substitute any flavor of broth, stock or even water.

PREP 20 MIN | COOK 3 MIN | NATURAL RELEASE

INGREDIENTS

2 carrots, diced

2 celery, diced

1/2 onion, diced

6 andouille sausages (13 oz)

3 Roma tomatoes, chopped

1 Cup basmati rice, rinsed

1 Cup chicken stock

1 Tablespoon Cajun seasoning

1/4 Teaspoon salt

INSTRUCTIONS

1. Combine all ingredients in the Instant Pot. Stir to combine.

2. Put lid on, set valve to sealing and Pressure Cook on High Pressure for 3 minutes. When cooking is complete, Naturally Release pressure.

3. Remove the lid and fluff rice with a fork.

Cheesy Broccoli & Rice

This Easy Cheesy Broccoli Rice is a fast and flavorful side when you don't have time to make a classic Broccoli Cheddar Casserole.

PREP 20 MIN | COOK 3 MIN | NATURAL RELEASE

INGREDIENTS

1-1/2 Cups jasmine rice

2 Tablespoons butter

2 Tablespoons minced onion

1 Tablespoon minced garlic

4 Cups chicken broth

3 Cups fresh or frozen broccoli florets

¾ Cup grated cheddar cheese

Salt and pepper to taste

INSTRUCTIONS

1. Turn on your Instant Pot to the Sauté setting.
2. When the display says HOT, add in the butter, minced onions, garlic & rice.
3. Sauté and stir for about 1 minute.
4. Add the broth and stir for 2 minutes, then add broccoli.
5. Cover the pot and secure the lid. Make sure the valve is set to sealing.
6. Select Pressure Cook at High Pressure for 10 minutes.
7. Once the rice is done cooking, Natural Release for 10 minutes and then Quick Release remaining pressure. Remove the lid.
8. Stir in the cheese, mix thoroughly.
9. Add salt and pepper to taste.

Cilantro Lime Rice

Bright and flavorful Cilantro Lime Rice! This is such an easy side dish that pairs perfectly with just about any Mexican dish, and it pairs well with seafood too.

PREP 5 MIN | COOK 17 MIN | NATURAL RELEASE

INGREDIENTS

14.5 Ounces chicken or vegetable broth

3/4 Cup water

2 Tablespoons canola oil

2 Limes*

2 Tablespoons fresh lime juice

2 Cups white long-grain rice

1/2 Cup cilantro, finely chopped

zest lime for garnish

INSTRUCTIONS

1. Add the broth, water, oil, lime juice, and long-grain rice into the Instant Pot. Stir.

2. Cover with lid making sure the vent is in the sealed position. Select Pressure Cook at High Pressure for 12 minutes.

3. Once cook time is over leave the rice in the Instant Pot for 5 minutes. Do a quick release for the remaining pressure. Fluff the rice.

4. Add chopped cilantro, zest & squeeze some juice of 1 lime into the rice and stir together to combine. Transfer rice to a serving bowl and Enjoy!

Notes

You will need 2 limes for this recipe. Once for the 2 Tablespoons inside the Instant Pot for the cook time, and one for when the rice is done as an add-in before serving.

COCONUT RICE

This easy coconut rice is rich, aromatic and delicious! Jasmine rice is mixed with coconut milk and a few aromatics to create the perfect side dish.

PREP 5 MIN | COOK 4 MIN | NATURAL RELEASE

INGREDIENTS

2 cups jasmine rice rinsed and drained

1 can coconut milk, full fat for a creamy rice

1 3/4 cups water

1 clove garlic minced

1 1/2 tsp salt or to taste

INSTRUCTIONS

1. After soaking rice for 20 minutes, rinse and drain well.
2. Add all the ingredients to the Instant Pot and stir well. Select Pressure Cook at High Pressure for 4 minutes.
3. Once cooking is complete. Naturally Release the pressure.
4. Open the lid, give it a good stir, and serve.

Fried Rice

This Chinese restaurant-style fried rice recipe is the absolute BEST. It's quick and easy to make, customizable with any of your favorite mix-ins, and so irresistibly delicious.

PREP 5 MIN | COOK 20 MIN | NATURAL RELEASE

INGREDIENTS

1 1/2 Cups Jasmine rice

4 Teaspoons vegetable oil, divided

1/2 Cup onions, finely chopped

2 Teaspoons ginger, finely minced

1 Tablespoon garlic, finely minced

3 Tablespoons soy sauce

1 Tablespoon oyster sauce

1/2 Teaspoon sesame oil

1/4 Teaspoon black pepper

1 1/2 Cups frozen peas and carrots

1 3/4 Cups water

2 eggs beaten

3 Tablespoons chopped green onions

INSTRUCTIONS

1. Select the Sauté function and allow the Instant Pot to heat up. Rinse and drain rice; set aside.

2. Add 1 Tablespoon vegetable oil to the Instant Pot inner pot. Add and sauté onions till translucent, about 2 minutes, stirring often.

3. Press Cancel. This will allow the Instant Pot to cool down while you do the next steps.

4. Sauté ginger and garlic for 30 seconds, stirring constantly. Stir in rinsed Jasmine rice until coated with onion mixture.

5. Deglaze inner pot with a tablespoon or two of water if there's anything stuck to the bottom.

6. Add soy sauce, oyster sauce, sesame oil, black pepper, frozen vegetables, and water. Stir to mix.

7. Close the lid, turn value to sealing, and Pressure Cook at High Pressure for 5 minutes.

8. Let the pressure Natural Release for 10 minutes and then release any remaining pressure using the Quick Release.

9. Open the lid and let the Fried Rice rest for a few minutes.

10. Heat a large nonstick frying pan over medium heat on the stove. Coat the frying pan with remaining vegetable oil and pour in the eggs.

11. Scramble the eggs by gently breaking up the eggs and flipping until eggs are set. Add eggs to the rice.

12. Add green onions and stir the rice gently to mix together all ingredients. Serve immediately.

Nick's Garlic Herb Chicken & Rice

I meal prep for my kids and this is my son's favorite to take for lunch. It's so easy to make and I know he is eating a good and hearty meal at school.

PREP 10 MIN | COOK 28 MIN | NATURAL RELEASE

INGREDIENTS

1 1/2 Cup Long Grain Basmati Rice

2 Cup Chicken Broth

1 Tablespoon Oil

2 Tablespoons Butter

1 large Onion

1 ½ Tablespoons Garlic Minced

1 ½ Tablespoons Italian Blend

1 Teaspoon Chili Powder

1 Tablespoon Paprika

Salt and Pepper to taste

Grated Parmesan to serve

6 Chicken Thighs, bone in

1 Teaspoon Chili Powder

1 Tablespoon Lemon Juice

1 Teaspoon Salt

1/2 Teaspoon Pepper

INSTRUCTIONS

1. Soak, wash and rinse rice.
2. Combine salt, pepper, chili powder, and lemon juice to form a paste. Cover chicken thighs all over with spice paste. Put to the side while you prepare the rest of ingredients.
3. Turn on the Instant Pot and select Sauté. Once heated add oil.
4. Add seasoned Chicken Thighs to the pot and sear 2-3 minutes on each side. Once they look light golden brown and crispy, remove and put aside.
5. Add butter and onion and sauté until onion looks soft and translucent.
6. Add Chopped garlic and cook for another 30 seconds. Add herbs, Paprika, Chili powder. Mix well.
7. Add soaked rice. Gently stir for 2-3 minutes roast rice.
8. Pour in Chicken Broth and season it with salt and pepper.
9. Arrange seared Chicken thighs in a single layer. Add any extra liquid that would have come from Chicken thigh while resting.
10. Select Pressure Cook and set the timer for 8 minutes.
11. When the timer is off, let the pressure release naturally for 8-10 minutes. Once the pressure is released completely, open the lid and let it rest for another 10 minutes.
12. Using a slotted spoon or fork separate rice grain gently.
13. While serving sprinkle with parsley and parmesan cheese to garnish.

Quinoa Taco Bowl

Quinoa Taco Bowls are healthy and delicious, combining the flavors of taco salad with the added benefits of quinoa, creating a dinner recipe that everyone is sure to love!

PREP 10 MIN | COOK 35 MIN | QUICK RELEASE

INGREDIENTS

1 Cup Quinoa, rinsed

1 1/4 Cup Water

1 Cup Salsa

2 Tablespoons Fresh Lime Juice

1 Teaspoon Garlic Powder

1 Teaspoon Oregano

1 Teaspoon Cumin

1 Teaspoon Chili Powder

1 Teaspoon Kosher Salt (1/2 Teaspoon table salt)

1/4 Teaspoon Pepper

1 (15 Ounce) can Black Beans, drained & rinsed

1 (15 ounce) can Corn, drained

For Toppings:

Cilantro

Avocado

Sour Cream

Jalapeño

Shredded Cheese

INSTRUCTIONS

1. Add all ingredients to the pressure cooker in order listed, except toppings, and place the lid on. Turn the valve to sealing position.

2. Select the Pressure Cook at High Pressure for 1 minute.

3. When the cook time has finished, turn off the pot and let it sit undisturbed for 15 minutes. Then Quick Release any remaining pressure.

4. Fluff with a fork and serve with any toppings you like.

Perfect Quinoa

*I've tried several quinoa cooking methods and this one works best.
It will come out fluffy every time.*

PREP 4 MIN | COOK 1 MIN | NATURAL RELEASE

INGREDIENTS

1 Cup dry quinoa

1 chicken broth

INSTRUCTIONS

1. Rinse quinoa under cold running water for about 1 minute. Drain.

2. Place quinoa and broth in Instant Pot. Close the lid and turn the valve to the sealing position.

3. Select Pressure Cook at High Pressure for 1 minute.

4. When the cook time has finished, Natural Release the steam. Carefully remove the lid.

5. Use a fork to fluff and separate the quinoa.

Rice Pilaf

Fluffy, flavorful, and fabulous, this easy rice pilaf recipe makes a great side dish all year long. The perfect side for any protein, and a regular in your dinner rotation.

PREP 10 MIN | COOK 3 MIN | NATURAL RELEASE

INGREDIENTS

- 1/4 Cup olive oil
- 1/3 Cup orzo
- 1 Cup white rice, rinsed
- 1 1/2 Cups chicken broth
- 1 Teaspoon garlic powder
- 3/4 Teaspoon coarse kosher salt
- 1/4 Teaspoon ground black pepper
- 1/4 Teaspoon onion powder
- 1/4 Teaspoon paprika
- 1 Tablespoon freshly parsley, chopped

INSTRUCTIONS

1. Turn Instant Pot on Sauté. Add the olive oil. Once hot, add orzo and cook for 2-3 minutes or until browned. Add the rice and cook until it turns bright white, about 3-4 minutes.

2. Carefully pour in the broth. Add garlic powder, salt, pepper, onion powder, and paprika. Cover pot and turn valve to sealing.

3. Cancel sauté and select Pressure Cook at High Pressure for 3 minutes. Once cooked, Natural Release the steam.

4. Open the lid and stir in the parsley. Let the rice sit for a few minutes before serving.

Risotto

Risotto is a northern Italian rice dish cooked with broth until it reaches a creamy consistency. The broth can be derived from meat, fish, or vegetables. Many types of risotto contain butter, onion, white wine, and parmesan cheese. It is one of the most common ways of cooking rice in Italy.

PREP 10 MIN | COOK 3 MIN | QUICK RELEASE

INGREDIENTS

4 Cups chicken broth

2 Tablespoons butter

1 medium onion, finely chopped

3 cloves garlic, minced

1 Tablespoon fresh thyme leaves

2 Cups Arborio rice

1/4 Cup dry white wine

3/4 Cup freshly grated Parmesan

Kosher salt

Freshly ground black pepper

INSTRUCTIONS

1. In a medium saucepan over medium heat, heat broth.

2. Set Instant Pot to Sauté and melt butter. Add onion and cook until soft, 5 minutes, then add garlic and thyme and cook until fragrant, 1 minute more. Add rice and stir until toasted, about 2 minutes.

3. Deglaze pot with wine, to scrap up the bits off the bottom. Cook until most of wine is absorbed, then turn Sauté function off.

4. Add warm broth and place lid on Instant Pot, turn valve to sealing. Select Pressure Cook at High pressure for 5 minutes.

5. Turn valve to Quick Release. Remove lid and stir in Parmesan. Season with salt and pepper to taste.

Turmeric & Garlic Rice

Here's a fun and healthy way to spice up your leftover rice so that it doesn't go to waste. Packed full of incredible flavors, this Turmeric Garlic Fried Rice dish is so easy to make and sure to please. Add a fried egg on top to round out your next meal.

PREP 2 MIN | COOK 25 MIN | NATURAL RELEASE

INGREDIENTS

1 Cup dry rice (Jasmine or Basmati white rice works best here)

1 Cup chicken broth

1 Tablespoon olive oil

1 Teaspoon turmeric

½ Teaspoon garlic powder

½ Teaspoon sea salt

Fresh cilantro, chopped for garnish

INSTRUCTIONS

1. Rinse the rice until the water runs clear. Shake out any excess liquid from the rice.

2. Add olive oil to the bottom of your instant pot.

3. Add rice to the pot. Sprinkle the turmeric, garlic powder, and sea salt over the rice, then add the broth. Give the pot a shake so that the rice is in one even layer.

4. Cover the pot, seal lid and turn valve to sealing. Select Pressure Cook at High Pressure for 6 minutes. Once the timer goes off, allow the pressure to Natural Release for 10 minutes.

5. Open the lid, Fluff with a fork, and serve warm with chopped cilantro.

Yummy Wild Rice

Wild rice is a beautiful, traditional food that often takes a long time to prepare. Instant Pot Wild Rice saves time and gives you perfect results every time!

PREP 0 MIN | COOK 35 MIN | NATURAL RELEASE

INGREDIENTS

2 cups dry wild rice

5 cups chicken broth

Salt & Pepper to Taste

INSTRUCTIONS

1. Add the wild rice and broth to the Instant Pot.
2. Place the lid on the Instant Pot and turn until it locks into place. Turn valve to sealing.
3. Select Pressure Cook at High Pressure for 35 minutes.
4. When cooking is complete, Natural Release pressure.
5. Open the lid immediately and fluff with a fork.
6. Add salt and pepper to your taste.

Yellow Rice with Peas & Corn

I love this rice recipe and it goes with just about any dish.

PREP 5 MIN | COOK 15 MIN | NATURAL RELEASE

INGREDIENTS

2 Cups basmati rice

3 Tablespoons olive oil

1 large onion, diced

1/4 Teaspoon salt

3 Tablespoons of fresh cilantro, chopped

2 large cloves of garlic, diced

1 heaping Teaspoon of turmeric powder

1 Cup frozen sweet corn kernels

1 Cup frozen garden peas

2 1/4 Cups chicken broth

1 Tablespoon of butter

INSTRUCTIONS

1. Rinse the rice remove some of the starch. This will help to keep the rice nice and fluffy.

2. Select the Sauté function on your pot. Add the olive oil, onions and salt and cook for 5 minutes, stirring a few times until softened.

3. Add the chopped cilantro, garlic and turmeric powder and stir. Add the corn, peas and rice and pour over the chicken broth. Stir and cancel sauté function.

4. Add the lid, turn valve to sealing. Select Pressure Cook at High Pressure for 4 minutes.

5. Once the timer goes off, turn the Instant Pot off and Natural Release for 5 minutes. Then Quick Release the rest of the steam.

6. Open the lid and add butter. Let it melt into the rice, then fluff it with a fork. Transfer to a serving platter.

Vegetable Recipes

It's difficult to think anything but pleasant thoughts
while eating a homegrown tomato.

-*Lewis Grizzard*

Bacon Brussel Sprouts

Kids and Brussel Sprouts… need I say more?
Add bacon and it's a whole new ballgame!

PREP 10 MIN | COOK 10 MIN | NATURAL RELEASE

INGREDIENTS

4 Strips bacon, chopped

1 Pound Brussel Sprouts, trimmed and halved lengthwise

1/4 Cup soy sauce

1/4 Cup apple cider vinegar

1/2 Teaspoon coarse Kosher salt

1/2 Teaspoon coarsely ground black pepper

INSTRUCTIONS

1. Select the Sauté function on the Instant Pot. When the display reads HOT, add chopped bacon and cook for about 5 minutes until crispy, stirring frequently. Turn off the sauté.

2. Add Brussel Sprouts, soy sauce, vinegar, salt, and pepper. Stir to mix well, using a wooden spoon to briefly scrape up any brown bits stuck to the bottom of the pot.

3. Secure and seal the lid. Select Pressure Cook at High Pressure for 4 minutes, followed by Natural Release.

4. Use a slotted spoon to scoop up the Brussel sprouts and bacon onto a serving plate.

Mashed Sweet Potatoes

Mashed Sweet Potatoes are a delicious change from our favorite mashed potatoes! With a creamy texture and delicious buttery flavor, they are the perfect side dish for any meal!

PREP 10 MIN | COOK 10 MIN | QUICK RELEASE

INGREDIENTS

2 Pounds sweet potatoes, peeled and cut into 1-inch pieces

1 Cup water

1 Tablespoon unsalted butter

1/2 Teaspoon cinnamon

1/8 Teaspoon kosher salt

ground nutmeg, a pinch or to taste

INSTRUCTIONS

1. Add sweet potatoes and water into the instant pot.
2. Make sure that the release valve is in the Sealing position. Place the lid on the Instant Pot, turn and lock.
3. Select Pressure Cook at high pressure for 10 minutes.
4. Once cook time is complete, carefully Quick Release the pressure from the pot.
5. Drain the potatoes and transfer them to a large bowl. Add butter, cinnamon, salt, and nutmeg to the potatoes.
6. Mash the potatoes using a potato masher until a smooth puree is created with some small chunks. Adjust seasonings as desired.

Roasted Butternut Squash

Roasted Butternut Squash is the perfect simple side dish or a great addition to salads, soups, or chili.

PREP 5 MIN | COOK 12 MIN | QUICK RELEASE

INGREDIENTS

2 Pounds butternut squash, peeled & cut into 1 inch cubes

1 Cup water

Salt & Pepper to taste

INSTRUCTIONS

1. Place your trivet or steamer basket into your Instant Pot. Add water and squash. Close lid and set valve to sealing.
2. Select Pressure Cook at High Pressure for 6 minutes.
3. When cooking complete, perform a Quick Release.
4. Open lid and cubes should be soft. You can serve as cubes or mix with immersion blender and puree.
5. Add salt & pepper to taste.

Fried Cabbage

This fried cabbage is cooked to tender perfection with bacon and onions. A super easy low carb side dish that's perfect for any occasion.

PREP 10 MIN | COOK 3 MIN | QUICK RELEASE

INGREDIENTS

2 Tablespoons olive oil

1/2 onion diced

3 Slices bacon

1 Cup vegetable broth

1 Head cabbage

1/2 Teaspoon garlic salt

1/2 Teaspoon salt

1/2 Teaspoon seasoned salt

1/2 Teaspoon paprika

1/2 Teaspoon chili powder

3 Tablespoons soy sauce

INSTRUCTIONS

1. Add olive oil, onions and diced bacon to your Instant Pot and Select Sauté.

2. Cook until bacon is done, not crispy done, but until meat is cooked. Add 1/4 cup of your vegetable broth and deglaze bottom of pot.

3. Cut cabbage into chunks, separate leaves and add into your pressure cooker.

4. Pour your remaining vegetable broth over cabbage leaves.

5. Sprinkle all spices and soy sauce on top of cabbage.

6. Stir gently to coat all leaves evenly.

7. Close lid and turn valve to sealing. Select Pressure Cook at High Pressure for 3 minutes (2 minutes if you want cabbage to be firmer).

8. When cooking is complete Quick Release pressure, remove lid and stir cabbage well.

9. Serve with your favorite entrée or with cornbread.

Coconut Curry Sweet Potatoes

This one-pot sweet potato coconut curry is bursting with sweet and spicy flavor. Grab a bowl and cozy on up with this fall-inspired dish.

PREP 10 MIN | COOK 20 MIN | QUICK RELEASE

INGREDIENTS

1 Tablespoon olive oil
1 onion, chopped
3-4 Cloves garlic minced
2 inch fresh ginger, minced
1 Cup tomato sauce
1 Pound sweet potatoes, peeled and chopped into 1 inch cubes
1 1/3 Cups canned coconut milk
15 ounce can of chickpeas, rinsed and drained
2 Cups fresh spinach
1/2 Tablespoon curry powder
1 Teaspoon ground turmeric
1 Teaspoon ground cumin
3/4 Teaspoon salt
1/2 Teaspoon smoked paprika
1/2 Teaspoon red pepper flakes
1/4 Teaspoon black pepper
1/4 Teaspoon ground ginger
Fresh herbs to garnish parsley and/or cilantro

INSTRUCTIONS

1. Add the oil to the Instant Pot and press Sauté.

2. Add the onion and sauté for about 3 minutes. Stir in garlic and fresh ginger and sauté for another 1 minute. Add all spices and stir again.

3. Next, add the tomato sauce, the sweet potato chunks, and the coconut milk.

4. Close the lid and turn value to seal. Select Pressure Cook on High Pressure for 2 minutes. Once cooking is complete, Quick Release the steam.

5. Carefully open the lid. Add chickpeas for additional protein.

6. Stir in the spinach and let simmer until wilted.

7. Taste and adjust seasonings. Add salt, pepper or crushed red pepper if needed.

8. Serve with rice and garnish with fresh herbs (cilantro or parsley for example).

Creamy Cheesy Au Gratin Potatoes

These homemade au gratin potatoes are always welcome at our dinner table, and they're so simple. I could have these every day.

PREP 15 MIN | COOK 25 MIN | NATURAL RELEASE

INGREDIENTS

3 Pounds white potatoes, peeled and sliced into 1/4 inch rounds

1 Cup chicken broth

1/2 Teaspoon salt

1/2 Teaspoon ground black pepper

1/2 Teaspoon oregano

1 Teaspoon garlic powder

4 Cloves garlic, minced

1 Cup heavy cream

2 Cups cheddar cheese, shredded and divided

INSTRUCTIONS

1. Add sliced potatoes to the Instant Pot.
2. Add broth, salt, pepper, oregano, and garlic powder, stir to combine.
3. Close the lid and turn valve to sealing. Select Pressure Cook on High Pressure for 1 minute, followed by a 3 minute Natural Release and Quick Release any remaining pressure.
4. Preheat oven to 375 degrees F.
5. Gently transfer the potatoes from the Instant Pot to a baking dish and set aside.
6. Select Sauté and add the garlic to the leftover liquid in the pot. Stir and cook for 30 seconds.
7. Add cream and let it slightly simmer. Turn off Instant Pot and add 1 cup of shredded cheese, stir until fully melted and smooth.
8. Pour the cheese sauce over the potatoes, toss to distribute and sprinkle on top the remaining 1 cup of shredded cheese.
9. Bake for 15 minutes, or until the mixture is bubbly. Broil for a few minutes to brown the top.
10. Potatoes will thicken as they start to cool.

Delicious Artichokes

These yummy artichokes are drizzled with a garlic butter sauce and garnished with fresh lemon and parsley.

PREP 10 MIN | COOK 8 MIN | QUICK RELEASE

INGREDIENTS

3 medium artichokes

1 Cup chicken broth

1 Teaspoon garlic powder

4 cloves garlic, minced

1/4 Cup unsalted butter, melted

1 Tablespoon lemon juice

Salt & ground black pepper

Fresh lemon

Chopped parsley for garnish

INSTRUCTIONS

1. Add artichokes to a large bowl and cover with cold water, let them sit for 5-10 minutes.

2. Remove from water, cut stem off, and trim the tip by about 1 inch. Remove any brown or wilted leaves.

3. Add broth and garlic powder to the Instant Pot and stir. Add a trivet or steamer rack and arrange the whole artichokes onto the trivet, tip of artichoke facing upwards.

4. Lock lid and turn valve to sealing.

5. Select Pressure Cook on High Pressure for 8 minutes followed by a Quick Release of steam.

6. Open the lid carefully and remove artichokes to a cutting board, slice in half if desired.

7. In a medium bowl, combine remaining ingredients and stir together.

8. Squeeze half a lemon over the artichokes, sprinkle salt to taste and spoon sauce over the artichokes.

9. Garnish with fresh parsley before serving.

Easy Golden Beets

This recipe will give you wonderful delicious golden beets ready for salads, making hummus, or throwing into smoothies. This mighty vegetable is high in fiber, potassium, and calcium; making it the perfect addition to a balanced diet.

PREP 5 MIN | COOK 26 MIN | NATURAL RELEASE

INGREDIENTS

2 Cups water

4 medium golden beets

INSTRUCTIONS

1. Rinse and scrub beets. Cut off leafy part.
2. Add 2 cups of water to the Instant Pot and place trivet or steamer basket into the Instant Pot.
3. Add beets, place lid and turn valve to sealing.
4. Select Pressure Cook on high pressure for 12 minutes for soft beets or 7 minutes for crunchy beets.
5. Once cooking is finished, allow to sit another 14 minutes to steam.
6. Use tongs to carefully remove beets from the Instant Pot.
7. Place beets on a cutting board and allow to cool to touch before removing skins.
8. Use a paper towel to remove skins and slice before serving.

Eggplant Parmesan

Perfect for Meatless Mondays, this easy eggplant parmesan recipe is not only delicious, but also healthy.

PREP 5 MIN | COOK 20 MIN | NATURAL RELEASE

INGREDIENTS

2 Large eggplant

2 Cups marinara sauce, divided

2 Cups mozzarella cheese, shredded

salt

For Serving:

fresh basil

red pepper flakes

parmesan cheese

INSTRUCTIONS

1. Cut off the top and the bottom of the eggplants and stand up straight. Slice eggplant lengthwise into 1/4-1/2 inch slices. Salt eggplant slices on both sides.

2. In your Instant Pot, add 1/2 cup of marinara sauce and spread out evenly on the bottom. Cover sauce with a layer of eggplant, covering the bottom as best you can. Add 1/2 cup of sauce and sprinkle with cheese. Continue layering the eggplant, sauce, and cheese in 3 layers

3. Close Instant Pot lid, make sure valve is set to sealing. Select Pressure Cook on high pressure for 10 minutes. Natural Release pressure when complete and carefully remove lid.

4. Cut into 4 equal pieces and top with optional toppings, such as basil, red pepper flakes and parmesan cheese.

Garlic Parmesan Cauliflower

Cauliflower is my favorite vegetable and this recipe will turn plain cauliflower into an irresistible side dish with a bit of garlic, and a scattering of Parmesan.

PREP 5 MIN | COOK 1 MIN | QUICK RELEASE

INGREDIENTS

1 head of Cauliflower

1 Cup of water

1/4 Cup butter, melted

1 clove garlic, minced

1 Teaspoon grated lemon zest

2 Tablespoons parsley chopped

1/4 Teaspoon salt

1/4 Teaspoon ground black pepper

2 Tablespoons parmesan cheese

INSTRUCTIONS

1. Trim leaves from cauliflower head and wash. Place on trivet in your Instant Pot with 1 cup of water.

2. Combine butter, garlic, lemon zest, parsley, salt and pepper. Brush mixture on top of cauliflower. Coat well.

3. Close the lid, turn valve to the sealing position and lock lid.

4. Select Pressure Cook at High Pressure for 1 minutes. When cooking complete, Quick Release the pressure.

5. For an extra crispy finish, carefully remove your cauliflower head & place on a baking sheet.

6. Sprinkle Parmesan cheese over the top and sides.

7. Place in the oven on broil until your cheese is starting to brown, about 5 minutes.

8. Serve immediately.

Glazed Carrots

This is a great recipe for people who don't love veggies. They are soft, sweet, and yummy. These carrots are a good way to get some extra Vitamin A.

PREP 2 MIN | COOK 4 MIN | NATURAL RELEASE

INGREDIENTS

- **2 Pounds baby carrots**
- **1/3 Cup butter**
- **1/2 Teaspoon salt**
- **1/3 Cup brown sugar**
- **1/2 Teaspoon ground cinnamon**
- **1/2 Cup water**

INSTRUCTIONS

1. Place carrots into the Instant Pot.
2. Add butter, salt, brown sugar, cinnamon and water.
3. Cover the pot and turn valve to sealing.
4. Select Pressure Cook on High Pressure for 4 minutes.
5. Once the carrots are done cooking, Natural Release pressure and remove lid.
6. Stir carrots and serve.

Lemon Rosemary Asparagus

I never thought I'd eat asparagus, much less my kids. But this recipe surprised us all and we've loved eating asparagus for years now.

PREP 2 MIN | COOK 1 MIN | NATURAL RELEASE

INGREDIENTS

1 bunch fresh asparagus

1 Cup chicken broth

4 Tablespoons butter

½ Teaspoon dried rosemary

1/4 Teaspoon salt

2-4 Teaspoon fresh lemon juice

1/4 Cup grated parmesan cheese

INSTRUCTIONS

1. To ensure your asparagus fit in the pot, trim ends.
2. Select Sauté. Add the chicken broth, rosemary and butter to the pot.
3. When the butter is melted and the water is hot, add the asparagus, laying half in the pot, and the other half crossways over the first layer.
4. Close the lid and set the steam release valve to sealing.
5. Select Pressure Cook on High Pressure for 1 minute for thicker stems or 0 minutes for thinner asparagus.
6. As soon as the cooking cycle is finished, Natural Release pressure.
7. Use tongs to gently take the asparagus out of the pot onto a plate.
8. Add the salt and lemon juice to the liquid in the pot. Taste and adjust salt and/or lemon juice as needed.
9. Stir in the parmesan and then spoon mixture over the asparagus.
10. Serve immediately.

Mashed Cauliflower

This cauliflower mash recipe is the perfect low-carb substitute to mashed potatoes. The secret to making steamed cauliflower smooth and creamy? The Sour Cream!

PREP 5 MIN | COOK 8 MIN | QUICK RELEASE

INGREDIENTS

1/2 Tablespoon olive oil

4 Cloves garlic, smashed

1 1/2 Cups chicken broth

1 Large head cauliflower, core removed and roughly cut into florets

1/2 Tablespoon butter

1 Tablespoon sour cream

1/2 Teaspoon salt

1/4 Teaspoon fresh ground pepper

1/2 Cup freshly grated parmesan cheese

1/2 Teaspoon chopped fresh chives plus more for garnish

INSTRUCTIONS

1. Select Sauté on Instant Pot.
2. Add olive oil to instant pot and on warm, Stir in smashed garlic cloves; stir until garlic is golden brown on all sides, about 1 minute.
3. Stir in chicken broth and cook for 1 minute.
4. Turn off the sauté function and place steamer basket inside your Instant Pot.
5. Transfer prepared cauliflower to the basket inside the Instant Pot.
6. Close the lid and set the valve to sealing.
7. Select Pressure Cook on high pressure for 3 minutes.
8. Quick Release pressure. Open up the lid half way and let stand 3 minutes.
9. Drain out all of the liquid and transfer the cauliflower and garlic to a food processor or blender. You can also put it in a large bowl and use a potato masher.
10. Add butter, sour cream, salt, and pepper to the blender and process until smooth and creamy. I recommend using the pulse function because you have more control over how creamy or chunky you want your mashed cauliflower.
11. Transfer the cauliflower mixture to a mixing bowl or serving dish.
12. Stir in parmesan cheese and chives. Taste for seasonings and adjust accordingly.
13. Garnish with fresh chives and serve.

Mashed Potatoes

These homemade mashed potatoes are perfectly rich and creamy, full of great flavor, easy to make, and always a crowd fave.

PREP 10 MIN | COOK 10 MIN | NATURAL RELEASE

INGREDIENTS

2 Pounds Russet potatoes, peeled and quartered

1/2 Cup water

1 Teaspoon salt

1/2 Cup

6 Tablespoons butter

1/2 Teaspoon black pepper

2 Tablespoons chives, chopped

Extra butter for serving

INSTRUCTIONS

1. Place the potatoes, water and salt in Instant Pot.

2. Put the lid on, turn the valve to sealing, Select Pressure Cook on high pressure for 10 minutes.

3. When the timer goes off, Natural Release the pressure.

4. Add the milk, butter and pepper to the Instant Pot. Use a potato masher to make the potatoes to desired consistency. You can add more milk if needed, one tablespoon at a time.

5. Alternatively, you can transfer the contents of the Instant Pot to a mixer to whip your potatoes.

6. Taste and add more salt if needed.

7. Spoon the potatoes into a serving bowl. Top with additional pats of butter and chives if desired.

Parmesan Ranch Corn-on-the-Cob

This delicious Corn-on-the-Cob is the ultimate summertime BBQ recipe. It's a super easy to make and healthy side dish that everyone will love!

PREP 5 MIN | COOK 5 MIN | QUICK RELEASE

INGREDIENTS

1 ½ Cups water

4 Teaspoons grated Parmesan cheese

4 Tablespoons butter

4 Teaspoons dry ranch seasoning mix

4 ears of corn

INSTRUCTIONS

1. Remove husks from corn. Place trivet in Instant Pot and add water.
2. Add corn, secure lid and turn valve to sealing. Pressure cook at High Pressure for 5 minutes.
3. When cooking is complete, Quick Release the pressure.
4. In a small bowl, microwave butter until melted, about 30 seconds. Mix in ranch mix and Parmesan cheese.
5. Brush mixture onto cooked corn and enjoy!

Superfood Kale

Perfectly cooked and ready in minutes!
This is the easiest way to add more kale into your diet!

PREP 3 MIN | COOK 3 MIN | QUICK RELEASE

INGREDIENTS

1 Pound kale

1/2 Cup water

2 Tablespoon extra-virgin olive oil

2 Cloves garlic minced

1/2 Teaspoon red pepper flakes (optional)

salt to taste

INSTRUCTIONS

1. Wash kale, the coarsely chop it and discard the stems.

2. Pour water in the Instant Pot and add kale. Close the lid and turn the valve to sealing. Select Pressure Cook at High Pressure for 3.

3. When cooking is complete, Quick Release the steam.

4. Drain kale and add it back to the Instant Pot. Select Sauté, then add olive oil and minced garlic.

5. For a spicier flavor, add red pepper flakes and mix with kale. (optional step)

6. Cook, stirring every 10 seconds, until garlic is fragrant, about 1 minute, and add salt to taste. Serve.

Perfectly Steamed Broccoli

Steamed broccoli can be enjoyed in so many ways. Mix it into a stir-fry, add into casseroles, or it can be a stand-alone side. The options are limitless.

PREP 5 MIN | COOK 5 MIN | QUICK RELEASE

INGREDIENTS

1 ½ Cups water

2 heads broccoli cut off stalks and into florets

2 Tablespoons butter melted

3 Tablespoons parmesan cheese, shredded

INSTRUCTIONS

1. Pour water into your Instant Pot and put vegetable steamer basket inside.
2. Wash broccoli, remove stalks, and cut crowns into bite size florets.
3. Place florets into steamer basket, close lid and turn steam valve to sealing. Select Pressure Cook at High Pressure for 1 minute for firmer broccoli or 2 minutes for very soft.
4. When cooking is complete, Quick Release the pressure, remove steamer basket, and place florets into a bowl.
5. While pressure is being released, melt butter in microwave about 20 seconds.
6. Pour melted butter on top of broccoli, stir to coat evenly, then add shredded parmesan to top. Serve immediately.

Steamed Spaghetti Squash

This is a good replacement for spaghetti noodles, or even just add some butter and garlic for a perfect side dish.

PREP 5 MIN | COOK 7 MIN | QUICK RELEASE

INGREDIENTS

1 Cup water

1 small to medium spaghetti squash cut in half, (widthwise)

INSTRUCTIONS

1. Pour water in bottom of Instant Pot.
2. Place Instant Pot trivet inside. Add Spaghetti Squash.
3. Put on lid, Turn valve to sealing. Select Pressure Cook at High Pressure for 7 minutes.
4. Quick Release the pressure.
5. Remove Spaghetti Squash from pot and use a fork to scrape squash out of skin.
6. Serve.

Spicy Garlic Zucchini

*This is a great recipe for all the garden zucchini that comes in.
It goes great with Italian dishes.*

PREP 5 MIN | COOK 5 MIN | QUICK RELEASE

INGREDIENTS

1 Cup water

4 Whole zucchini, cut into 1/2 inch pieces

2 Teaspoon olive oil

2 cloves garlic minced

1/2 Cup tomato sauce

1/2 Teaspoon red pepper flakes

1/2 Teaspoon Italian herb seasoning

1/2 Teaspoon salt

INSTRUCTIONS

1. Place zucchini and water in the Instant Pot. Close the lid and turn the valve to sealing. Select Pressure Cook at High Pressure for 2 minutes on High pressure.

2. When done cooking, Quick Release the steam and drain zucchini in a colander.

3. Add olive oil and minced garlic to the Instant Pot and press Sauté. When the garlic starts sizzling (in about 1 minute), add drained zucchini, tomato sauce, salt, red pepper flakes and Italian seasoning, Mix well until combined. Add salt to taste if needed.

4. Continue to cook for 2 minutes, then remove to a serving dish.

5. Serve immediately.

Steamed Veggie Mix

Pot Steamed Vegetables are super easy to make and only require a pressure cook time of zero minutes - yes, you read that correctly! Follow this no-fail method for perfect veggies every time.

PREP 10 MIN | COOK 0 MIN | QUICK RELEASE

INGREDIENTS

1 Cup chicken broth

1 Head broccoli, chopped

1 Head cauliflower, chopped

2 Whole carrots, chopped

1 red pepper, chopped

1 yellow pepper, chopped

½ Teaspoon garlic powder

¼ Teaspoon salt

¼ Teaspoon pepper

INSTRUCTIONS

1. Add chicken broth to the Instant Pot and then place trivet inside the inner pot. Add veggies, place lid on pot and turn valve to sealing.

2. Select Pressure Cook on High Pressure, then cook for 0 minutes. Yes, zero minutes is all that's needed to steam! The Instant Pot will take about 5-10 minutes to come to pressure, then notify you it's done by beeping.

3. Quick Release pressure and open lid carefully.

4. Stir in garlic powder, salt and pepper.

5. Serve.

Twice-Baked Potatoes

Twice Baked Potatoes are now fast and easy thanks to the Instant Pot! The potatoes are perfectly cooked every time. The insides are soft and fluffy, perfect for the twice baked potato filling!

PREP 10 MIN | COOK 20 MIN | NATURAL RELEASE

INGREDIENTS

8 small/medium russet potatoes

1 Cup chicken broth

1/4 Cup butter

1/4 Cup sour cream

1/4 Cup milk

1/4 Cup chives, chopped fine

1/2 Cup bacon crumbles

1/2 Cup cheddar cheese, shredded

salt and pepper to taste

INSTRUCTIONS

1. Wash and cut each potato in half, lengthwise. Place the potatoes in steamer basket or on trivet.

2. Pour the chicken broth into the Instant Pot. Place the steamer basket with the potatoes into the Instant Pot, or stack the potatoes onto the trivet.

3. Pressure cook on High Pressure for 10 minutes. The potato halves should fit in your hand easily. If your potatoes are larger, the cook time will need to be increased by about 5 minutes.

4. Naturally Release the pressure and remove the potatoes.

5. Hold each potato half in your hand with a dish towel and gently spoon out the inside of the potato into a bowl. Repeat with all potato halves.

6. Set the potato skins aside.

7. Add the butter, milk, and sour cream to the bowl with the potatoes. Mash with potato masher or mixer.

8. Fold the chives, bacon and shredded cheese into the mashed potatoes.

9. Spoon the mashed potato filling into each potato skin and line in an oven safe dish.

10. Broil until the tops of the potatoes are golden brown. Usually about 5 minutes, depending on your oven.

11. Serve immediately. Store leftovers in the fridge.

Zucchini Noodles

Perfect for hot summer evenings or when you simply don't have the energy or will to turn up the stove. It's light, healthy and only takes minutes.

PREP 5 MIN | COOK 2 MIN | Saute' Only

INGREDIENTS

2 large zucchinis cut with a spiralizer

2 garlic cloves

1/2 lemon, juiced

3 Tablespoons parmesan cheese, grated

2 Tablespoons olive oil

salt and pepper to taste

1/2 Cup fresh basil, chopped

INSTRUCTIONS

1. Pour olive oil into your Instant Pot and add minced garlic.

2. Press Sauté function and cook for 1 minute, then add zucchinis, lemon juice and salt to taste.

3. Sauté for 30 seconds, so that zucchini remains firm.

4. Mix well and serve your zucchini noodles sprinkled with grated parmesan cheese and fresh basil.

Electric Pressure Cooker Information

Liquid Ingredients by Volume

1/4 tsp	=	1 ml	=			
1/2 tsp	=	2 ml	=			
1 tsp	=	5 ml	=			
3 tsp	=	1 tbl	=	1/2 fl oz	=	15 ml
2 tbls	=	1/8 cup	=	1 fl oz	=	30 ml
4 tbls	=	1/4 cup	=	2 fl oz	=	60 ml
5 1/3 tbls	=	1/3 cup	=	3 fl oz	=	80 ml
8 tbls	=	1/2 cup	=	4 fl oz	=	120 ml
10 2/3 tbls	=	2/3 cup	=	5 fl oz	=	160 ml
12 tbls	=	3/4 cup	=	6 fl oz	=	180 ml
16 tbls	=	1 cup	=	8 fl oz	=	240 ml
1 pt	=	2 cups	=	16 fl oz	=	480 ml
1 qt	=	4 cups	=	32 fl oz	=	960 ml
			=	33 fl oz	=	1000 ml = 1 liter

Dry Ingredients by Weight

1 oz	=	1/16 lb	=	30 g
4 oz	=	1/4 lb	=	120 g
8 oz	=	1/2 lb	=	240 g
12 oz	=	3/4 lb	=	360 g
16 oz	=	1 lb	=	480 g

Length comparisons

1 in	=			2.5 cm		
6 in	=	1/2 ft	=	15 cm		
12 in	=	1 ft	=	30 cm		
36 in	=	3 ft	=	1 yd	90 cm	
40 in	=			100 cm	=	1 m

Tips & Information Before Starting

Read through all instructions provided with your electric pressure cooker. Each brand or model could have slight differences, but overall functions are the same.

What is Pressure Cooking?

It is cooking food, using a liquid, with pressure in an airtight container. Steam is created by the pressure and cooks the food faster than traditional methods.

How to Release Pressure From the Instant Pot

Natural Release (NR) is to allow the pressure to release on its own. Depending on amount of food cooking will determine release time. It can range 5 to 40 minutes.

Quick Release (QR) is to turn the value from sealing to venting position and the steam will release. Use caution from steam. It WILL burn you.. trust me...

Liquid Amounts and Types

In order to build the pressure needed for cooking, the inner pot must have at least 1/2 to 1 cup of liquid. I personally always use 1 cup, so I always know I will have enough and not worry with the BURN light coming on.

The most common liquids to use are water, broths or stocks. Chicken, beef and vegetable broths or stocks work great. I normally use Chicken Broth, even if the recipe calls for water, because I like the flavor it adds to most anything I'm cooking. So, feel free to interchange them in your recipes to see which you like best.

Warm Up Time

The Instant Pot takes about 10 minutes to build the necessary pressure within the inner pot, so take that time into account when you are preparing meals.

Using Other Pans Inside Instant Pot

You can use Springform pans, Pyrex dishing or any oven baking safe dishes inside your Instant Pot. You would use these for example, Meatloaf and Mashed Potatoes recipe. You would put your potatoes in the bottom, place in your trivet and then meatloaf in oven safe pan on top of trivet. It gives you a stacking effect and the ability to cook a whole meal at once. The idea is to keep foods you don't want mixing together separated during cooking.

Foods Not to Cook

There are a few foods that do not cook well and should be left to other cooking methods. Foods that have a crispy or browned exterior, meats that you prefer to eat rare and easily overcooked seafood.

Safety and Cleaning

The Safety Tips I always follow:

- Never Fill to the Max for Pressure Cooking.
- Don't Deep Fry.
- Stay Away From the Steam.
- Replace the Sealing Ring When Necessary.

Be careful with the lid

Locking the lid properly is important before any pressure cooking. A lid that's off kilter or unlocked can explode off and cause burns. Talk about a hot mess!

Always double-check that the sealing ring is properly in position under the lid, clean, and free of debris before cooking. Otherwise, your lid may not seal correctly.

Finally, twist the lid clockwise and align the arrow with the locked icon to get the pot to lock properly. Your display should flash "Lid" if it isn't placed correctly.

Respect the Steam

Don't put any exposed body part over the steam valve unless you want a nasty burn. Be sure to keep your Instant Pot out of the reach of children, too. I "forget" and have burned myself more than a few times. It's totally a "user" problem. Please be careful.

Cleaning Your Instant Pot

Be sure to read all the recommendation in your manual. All I do to keep mine clean is after every cook, I empty the pot immediately and at LEAST fill it with dish soap and water. That way nothing sticks to it and there's no major scrubbing to do, which can scratch the inside. I wash it out and put it on the dish towel to dry. I wipe the rest of the appliance down with a damp wash cloth and that's it. I do that each use and I've never had any issues. Easy enough.

Make sure to remove the Condensation Collector from the back and clean every few uses. It will fill up and is easy to forget about.

Most of the Instant Pot's parts, including the inner pot and steam rack, can be washed in the dishwasher, making for a very straightforward and time-saving clean-up process. So pretty much, whichever way is easier and faster for you.. DO IT!

Author's Note

Thank you so much for reading *Instant Pot® Cookbook: Instant Dinner Recipes for Busy Lifestyles*. I hope you have picked several recipes to try and love them as much as I do! Together we can tackle dinner *one recipe at a time*.

Join our Facebook Community https://www.facebook.com/livingthechaos and share photos of your favorites! I love to see your personal touches!

Would you like to be the first to hear about my latest news? Please sign up for my author newsletter. I'll send them out whenever I have news at www.bitsykeown.com

My newsletter will be packed full of survival tips, additional recipes, and discount book offers.

If you loved this book, keep an eye out for the upcoming
Instant Pot® Cookbook Series:

Book 2 Quick and Easy Soups

Filled full of recipes for soups that warm the soul, during these cold days. Spending hours making homemade soups will be a thing of the past.

Book 3 MORE Main Meals

...More recipes to add variety to your dinners.

Book 4 After Dinner Desserts

Dessert recipes that can be cooking while you eat dinner

Book 5 The Leftovers

Learn to love leftovers and make them beautiful again.

I look forward to connecting with you! If you enjoyed this book, please leave a quick review on Amazon.

Manufactured by Amazon.ca
Bolton, ON